"In healthcare, trust is foundational. Trust is directly proportional to the leaders and team members' individual and collective levels of integrity, authenticity, vulnerability, and transparency. Quality, safety, performance, and most importantly patient outcomes are elevated in organizations that exhibit high levels of trust. *The Trust Circle* offers a road map and practical framework for leaders to build the relational strength and resiliency in their teams that is required to successfully navigate the complexity, urgency, and importance of our work in healthcare today."

—Chris Nicholas
COO Renown Health, CEO Renown Regional Medical Center

"Dr. Hallak's focus on 'relational investors' and the essential role for real human connection is an important antidote to this era of loneliness and frictionless technology to meet every need. Full of relatable examples and useful activities, Dr. Hallak walks the reader through the mindset and actions to build a robust, thriving professional community of 'relationship investors' for leaders and beyond."

—Alexis Fink
Senior Research Scientist, Former VP, People Analytics
and Workforce Strategy, Meta

"This book will transform the way you think about leadership networking. Where other people focus on what you can get, Daniel talks about trust and partnerships—giving and receiving, the chance to build a web of people who make each other better. You'll discover that building a leadership network isn't scary, but an exciting adventure; a chance to build a world where we bring out the best in others and discover our own hidden potential along the way."

—Paul R. Yost, PhD.
Co-author of Real-time Leadership Development and
Experience-Driven Leader Development

"As a president and active participant in a Convene peer group, I deeply believe in the value of trusted relationships in leadership. Daniel Hallak captures that truth powerfully in *The Trust Circle*. His message resonates because it reflects what many leaders learn the hard way: the weight of leadership was never meant to be carried alone. Hallak offers a clear and practical framework for building the right circle of people around you, people who challenge you, support you, and help position you wisely for what is next.

What I appreciate most about this book is that it is both insightful and actionable. It speaks directly to leaders navigating growth, transition, and responsibility, and it reinforces something I have experienced personally: meaningful peer relationships and intentional advisory circles make better leaders and healthier organizations. *The Trust Circle* is a timely and worthwhile read for any leader who wants to lead with greater clarity, resilience, and long-term impact."

—Josh Wylie
President at Villara Building Systems

"Daniel Hallak doesn't just study relational investment, he practices it. I've watched him pour into emerging leaders and been a recipient of the generosity he describes in these pages, which is why I trust what he's written. *The Trust Circle* gives the leader who can sense the need for change a vocabulary, an architecture, and the honest diagnostic tools to do it before the drift toward isolation becomes the path and derailment the cost. This is both serious scholarship and a genuine act of investment in the next generation of leaders."

—Glen Prior
Chief Operating Officer, Eden: People+Planet

"This book is a powerful reminder that we were never meant to lead alone. Daniel reinforces that leadership is ultimately about people and purpose, calling us to move beyond self-sufficiency and intentionally build a circle of relationships that strengthen us. *The Trust Circle* provides a framework for prioritizing relationships so we can serve with endurance and make a greater impact."

—Tim Neville
President/CEO, Echoing Hills Village Inc.

"Dr. Daniel Hallak perceives people, really perceives them. This goes beyond mere listening with one's ears, or bringing empathy to a conversation. It ties to seeing a person's worth, not just an individual, but as someone who sits within a network of valuable relationships. His message is one of investing in these networks for an ROI that blesses entire enterprises: people and culture, with long-tail effects.

If you are looking for a way to bypass networking, you won't find it here. What you will find is the construct for intentional relational investment. This book holds wisdom. I will be putting it in the hands of others learning to develop their circle of trust."

—Mark L. Vincent
The Maestro-Suite of Executive Advising | Sage Group
Collective Founding Member and Facilitator

"I had the privilege of both working professionally with Daniel while pursuing a PhD alongside him. During a prolonged and demanding season of life, I had a front-row seat to view him in action. I can say without reservation that Daniel is one of the wisest and most honorable leaders I know. What he shares in this intelligent book is both research-based and highly practical. There is no better guide to building a community of relational investors than Dr. Hallak. He has been a source of stretch, support, and strategic input for me, and will be for you, too, as you invest time in *The Trust Circle*."

—John R. Terrill
Executive Director, SL Brown Foundation

"I love this notion of a 'relational investor'—as it's a double entendre. It could be an adjective— as we think about placing assets, but in this case it's a verb—a mindset, put to action, which will indeed provide a great 'return.' But, the return may be MUCH more than expected; in a world with a transactional mindset, Dr. Daniel Hallak calls leaders to be relational—in their approach with co-workers, but also in creating a team through a relational ecosystem."

—Jeff Rogers
Chair, Park Place Motors & OneAccord

"In an increasingly digital world, Dr. Hallak brings us back to what matters most: human connection. Through the concept of the 'trust circle,' he thoughtfully illustrates how leaders can build and sustain meaningful relationships with both authenticity and intention. He writes with a rare blend of data-driven insight and lived experience, offering a clear and actionable framework for leaders who are serious about long-term success. This is more than a book; it's a manual for building the relational foundation every leader needs. A must-read, and more importantly, a must revisit."

—Nicole Petersen, MA
Director of People Development, Renown Health

"As an executive career coach who has seen thousands of leaders both at their best, and their worst, I instantly recognized a great many of the themes that Daniel has called out—and salute him for providing practical, detailed, and highly illustrative examples of both good and bad leadership behaviors in action to help all of us take these lessons to heart. As my own personal mentor used to say, back when I started my own career in 1993, some lessons about business success can be taught, while some lessons can "only be caught" through personal experience. In this masterful book, however, Daniel does his best to blur this distinction by sharing the hard-won lessons he's gained through his own extensive work with successful leaders—and smart leaders would be well-served to "catch" some of the key principles he's laid out in this outstanding effort."

—Matt Youngquist
Executive Career Coach, Career Horizons

"In *The Trust Circle*, Daniel Hallak captures something most leadership books miss: you don't succeed alone, and you don't last alone. He offers a practical framework for building the relationships that shape a leader's effectiveness—those who stretch you, support you, and open doors. From the self-assessment up front to the specific tools and real-world examples, *The Trust Circle* is a must-read for any leader serious about having an impact over the long term."

—George Noroian
President, Giant Leap

"Decades of research tells us that relationships shape healthy, resilient leaders. *The Trust Circle* brings this to life by showing how to build a circle of 'relational investors'—people who know you, challenge you, and walk with you—so you're not leading alone."

—Dr. Denise Daniels, Hudson T. Harrison
Professor of Entrepreneurship at Wheaton College

"Daniel has created something truly valuable with *The Trust Circle*. His approach reflects what I've spent decades helping executives understand: leaders succeed when they intentionally cultivate relationships around them. He highlights the risks of building relationships and more importantly the risks of trying to lead alone. The book isn't just descriptive, it's prescriptive, on how you can build stronger and more resilient teams and sustainable leadership capacity. This book should be read by every leader!"

—Michael Erisman
Principal at Talent Realized, Former Vice President and General Manager, Global Human Resources at DocuSign

THE
TRUST
CIRCLE

THE TRUST CIRCLE

UNLOCK THE POWER OF RELATIONSHIPS TO LEAD WITH IMPACT

DANIEL HALLAK, PhD

WILEY

Published by John Wiley & Sons, Inc., Hoboken, New Jersey.

For general information on our other products and services or for technical support, please contact our Customer Care Department within the United States at (800) 762-2974, outside the United States at (317) 572-3993 or fax (317) 572-4002.

Wiley also publishes its books in a variety of electronic formats. Some content that appears in print may not be available in electronic formats. For more information about Wiley products, visit our website at www.wiley.com.

Library of Congress Cataloging-in-Publication Data is Available:

ISBN 9781394379309 (Cloth)
ISBN 9781394379316 (ePub)
ISBN 9781394379323 (ePDF)

COVER DESIGN: PAUL MCCARTHY
COVER IMAGE: © GETTY IMAGES | FLAVIO COELHO

Printed and bound by CPI Group (UK) Ltd, Croydon, CR0 4YY
C9781394379309_010626

To the love of my life, my wife, Kristin. This book wouldn't be possible without you. You are always there for me, and you've helped me to do things I only could have dreamed of. You've stretched me, supported me, and helped me strategically like no one else. You are the spice of my life and my sweetest gift.

Contents

PART IV   Strategy   **127**

Foreword

By Dr. Rob McKenna

Leadership can be many things. It can be energizing and purposeful, filled with possibility and momentum. But if we are honest, leadership can also be lonely. Many leaders carry more responsibility than they ever expected. They shoulder decisions that affect families, organizations, and communities. They are asked to move forward with clarity and conviction while navigating uncertainty and complexity. And far too often they do it with far less support than they need.

Leaders don't fail first because of strategy, execution, pressure, or complexity. Leaders fail first in isolation.

Over the years I have spent much of my work studying trust and leadership—how trust is built, how it is broken, and how it shapes the lives of individuals, teams, and organizations. One pattern appears again and again in both research and real life: leadership was never meant to be a solo thing. The strongest leaders are rarely the most independent ones. They are the most connected. If we are not surrounded, we are alone—and when leaders are alone long enough, something begins to fracture from the inside out.

That is why this book matters. In *Circle of Trust*, Dr. Daniel Hallak reveals something many leaders intuitively know but rarely cultivate intentionally—the circle of relationships that surrounds a leader and sustains them over time. In these pages he calls those relationships relational investors: people who stretch us, support us, and strategically position us for the defining moments of leadership. Daniel has spent his career advising leaders during pivotal transitions—moments of scale, succession, sale, and reinvention. What he has seen again and again is unmistakable: leaders who last do not lead alone. They build circles of people who help them see more clearly, grow more honestly, and endure more faithfully. Leadership strength is never simply about the individual leader. It always includes the people who surround that leader.

My own journey studying leadership and trust has often led me back to a simple image: the circle. For more than a decade I have noticed small metal washers—a simple circle—showing up everywhere: on sidewalks, in gutters, in places most people would never look twice. When I see one, I pick it up. Each one has become a quiet reminder of something essential about leadership. A circle represents wholeness. It reminds me that leadership is not merely about performance or position but about becoming a more integrated person over time. Yet we pursue that wholeness in the midst of fragmentation and brokenness, both within ourselves and in our relationships with others. The circle reminds me that leadership is not about pretending we are whole, but about pursuing wholeness while acknowledging the fractures that exist in every human life and every relationship.

But the circle carries another meaning as well. It reminds me to think about the long haul. Leadership is not only about what we accomplish in the moment we occupy today. The relationships we invest in now shape a future that will outlive us. The trust we extend, the leaders we develop, and the people we invest in ripple outward into years and generations we may never see. Long after our names are forgotten, the people we invested in will still be investing in others. Leadership that lasts is rarely built through individual brilliance. Leadership that lasts is built through relational investments over time.

That perspective changes how we think about relationships themselves. It is not enough simply to have mentors or a few trusted friendships. Lasting leadership requires something more intentional: a network of relationships that surround us with purpose—different people who challenge us, support us, and guide us through different seasons of life and leadership. A leader without those relationships may still succeed for a while, but they will not last.

Leadership without relational support eventually collapses under its own weight.

This is precisely the insight Daniel develops so powerfully in this book. Research in psychology and leadership has long demonstrated the importance of social support. Over time that research has become more precise, helping us understand that leaders need different kinds of relationships for different purposes—relationships that stretch us, support us, and position us strategically for the challenges ahead. Daniel has lived and breathed that work throughout his career, and this book translates those insights into something every leader can understand and apply.

More importantly, Daniel does not simply teach this concept—he lives it. He is one of the most intentional relational connectors I know. But what makes Daniel unique is that his relationships are never merely strategic or transactional. They are deeply personal. He brings people together with a genuine commitment to their flourishing. The connections he cultivates are purposeful, generous, and grounded in the belief that leadership is always strengthened through relationships.

I have had the privilege of watching Daniel develop this work over many years. Few things are more meaningful to a leader than seeing the ideas and investments of one generation carried forward and strengthened by the next. Daniel represents that kind of continuation for me—a leader I have had the privilege of investing in and walking alongside for many years, who has taken these convictions about relationships, trust, and leadership and translated them into a framework that will serve leaders for generations.

In my own work, including my book *Whole Leaders, Wild Trust*, I wrote about the importance of leaders being intentionally surrounded—developing networks of support that help them grow into whole and trustworthy leaders over time. Daniel's work brings that idea to life with clarity and practicality. He shows leaders not only why these relationships matter but how to build them.

And the timing of this book could not be more important. We live in a time when leaders are under enormous pressure and many feel increasingly isolated. But isolation is not a leadership strategy—it is a leadership risk. The leaders who endure, the leaders who finish well, are the leaders who refuse to lead alone.

In these pages you will discover a framework for building the relationships that help leaders last. You will learn how to surround yourself with people who stretch your thinking, support you in difficult seasons, and strategically position you for the opportunities ahead. But more importantly, you will be challenged to become that kind of relational investor for others. Because the true measure of leadership is not the success we achieve alone—it is the leaders we help build around us.

Daniel Hallak has given leaders an extraordinary gift in this book: a blueprint for building the relationships that sustain leadership for the long run. Read it carefully. Apply it intentionally. Build your circle. Because leadership is too important—and too demanding—for any of us to attempt it alone.

Dr. Rob McKenna
Founder and CEO, WiLD Leaders
National Best Selling Author of *Whole Leaders, Wild Trust*

Introduction: Leaders Who Last

What is the secret to lasting leadership? We all want the magic formula. I've spent my career advising leaders on human capital, culture, and leadership to create highly differentiated value. I'm a student of leadership, and I've always been hungry to learn from effective leaders who are making a meaningful impact in the world. In my work I'm usually invited to help create organizational alignment, clarity, and trust, as an owner gets ready for scale, sale, or succession. It's a moment that matters, a critical inflection point for these leaders and their teams. They know that they need help navigating change, and they have a lot of questions. What's the right strategy? How do we align our team? What systems and processes do we need to optimize? How do I know if I've prepared my successor to take over? Is my business sellable? Is this the right position for the business? Am I ready? What should I do next? What comes after this? These are some of their honest questions.

These leaders are in a moment that could make or break their business, their career, and their legacy. They want to get it right. But that's not all they want. They want to create something of lasting value that outlives them. They want to leave the people in their business better than they found them. It's not just business; it's personal.

These leaders have invited me into their lives and their work. I've learned a lot from them, and I've seen unmistakable patterns across industries. As I work with them, I'm left inspired, but I'm fascinated the most with the leader who has finished their race well—the leaders who last. They have experienced it all—the highs and the lows, the insurmountable and the unbelievable. They have successfully grown and scaled businesses. They have navigated the twists and turns of selling to the right buyer. They have created leadership continuity by careful succession planning with the next generation of ownership. The leaders who last have worked hard and put in the hours. The ones I want to emulate have intentionally attended to leading well across their whole lives: at home, in their workplaces, and in their communities.

Block or Unlock Value

There are proven strategies, models, and tools to navigate complexity and create value. The leaders who last put them to practice. But that's not what makes them great. It takes something different to become a leader who lasts. Lasting leaders have discovered the factor that can block or unlock value during a critical moment of scale, sale, or succession: YOU. Your personal health and effectiveness are the difference makers in navigating transitions successfully. Leaders who last are the leaders who prioritize relationships with people who keep them on track across their whole lives. The enduring theme I've observed in the lives of leaders who navigate transitions well and stand the test of time is that they don't lead alone. The leaders who last for the long term surround themselves with the right people; they have a circle of highly intentional relationships that develop them and drive them. This is what I call the trust circle in this book.

These remarkable leaders have discovered the relational secret to success. They realized that they needed a circle of support if they were going to have the sustained energy to keep leading and serving, especially in the defining moments of their businesses and their careers. They are intentional about surrounding themselves with relational investors, other leaders who are committed to helping them become successful now and in the future.

Relational Investors

Your relational investors make up your trust circle. It's a development circle, what many people would describe as your personal board of advisors.[1] Relational investors are committed to your growth, health, and success. Lasting leaders have a circle of relational investors who invest in them in three different ways, bringing them stretch, support, and strategy.

When I meet these relationally grounded leaders, I pay close attention. Like them, I want to be a leader who lasts. I want to practice the relational secret to sustainable leadership. I want to look back at the end of my career and my life and see a meaningful and positive impact from leading in my family, in my work, and in my community. I need relational investors, and I want to be one myself.

Every day I see leaders who are isolated, lonely, and burning out. The impact of their lonely leadership negatively affects their families and communities. Eventually, these leaders get derailed, or they give up. The growth and scale of their business becomes stagnate. They pass the baton for their business too soon, and their successors aren't prepared to lead at the next level. They rush a sale without careful alignment between their vision and the buyers. The stakes are too high to lead alone. There is a desperate need for leaders to get the relational support that is necessary to sustain themselves for the long term.

Is This Your Moment?

This book is written for you if you are a leader who is in or going into a critical inflection point, a moment of transition that could make or break your business, your career, and your legacy. You want your business to flourish and create long-term value for your entire ecosystem of employees, customers, partners, suppliers, and even the broader community that you touch.

This book is written to be an inspirational and practical field guide for getting the right support, from the right people, at the right moments. My intent is to invest in you to become a leader who stands the test of time. I want you to become a relational investor who pours into the next generation of leaders after you. To navigate inflection points successfully, you need a circle of advisors—leaders who can help you successfully navigate scale, sale, or succession by stretching you, supporting you, or positioning you strategically. You are what gets in the way or what gets the deal done. You can't lead alone.

I've written this book to pass on the relational keys to career and leader success that I've learned from leaders who last. The secret of the relational investors in this book can breathe life into your work and inspire you to live with greater intentionality, deeper relational connection, and more abundant generosity both in your work but also throughout your whole life.

Is It Your Turn to Lead?

I also wrote this book for the emerging leader who wants to lead at the next level. You are the future leader who is going to take over the family business, continuing a legacy that's bigger than you. You are an entrepreneur who is growing a significant enterprise, and you want your personal capacity to scale at the same rate as your organization. You are figuring it out along the way, and you need a tribe of guides. If you've picked up this book, then you probably realize that the stakes for leading are high and you want to learn how to lead well for the long term. You have people who are relying on you, and you have expectations for yourself as well.

The critical ingredient to becoming a leader who lasts for the long term is a circle of relational investors who give you stretch, support, and strategy. It's likely that you already have those relationships, but you've never taken the steps to activate their full investment. As you read this book, you'll be inspired to get surrounded by generous relational investors. As you do, I challenge you to consider what it would take for you to become that generous relational investor for someone else, passing along what you receive.

Don't Lead Alone

I've approached this book from three perspectives. As a leader who is in process myself, I'm drawing on my personal experiences of having leaders generously invest in me. As a social scientist, I'm extracting wisdom from the decades of research in the psychological and organizational sciences. As a strategic advisor who guides leaders in a path to value, I'm tapping into the real stories of leaders who are working to serve the people in their care (details about identities sometimes masked or altered for confidentiality). You'll find real stories, new ways of thinking, and practical tools and self-assessments to help you get the relational investors you need to stand the test of time and successfully lead through scale, sale, or succession.

In the rest of this book, you'll build a road map for moving from isolation to connection. You can read every chapter in order, or you can choose your own adventure and read the chapters you need, right when you need them. Here's how to get the most out of this book:

- **Avoid the Isolation Trap:** In the next chapter (Chapter 1) we'll look at the dangers of isolation and see how easy it is to become disconnected and lonely as a leader. You'll learn why your circle of relational investors is so critical to your long-term success.
- **Start with Intentionality:** In the following chapter (Chapter 2) I'll show you how to get more intentional about identifying relational investors. I'll also introduce the three primary categories of relational investors that you need so that you can become a leader who lasts: relationships for stretch, support, and strategy:
  - **Stretch:** In Part II we'll look at relationships that *stretch* you to your next level. These are people who give you honest *feedback* about what you do (Chapter 4) and offer *perspective* you don't have on your situation (Chapter 5).

- **Support:** In Part III we'll learn about relationships that *support* us. Some of these people give us *emotional support* when the storms of life threaten to overwhelm us (Chapter 6). Others are *mentors* who give us counsel along the paths of our journey (Chapter 7).
- **Strategy:** In Part IV we'll examine relationships that are *strategic.* These include *career connections* to new career opportunities (Chapter 8) and *advocates* who vouch for us and lobby for us before people with power (Chapter 9).

- **Become a Generous Relational Investor:** Leaders regularly tell me that they want a personal board of advisors but that building intentional connections makes them feel guilty that they are taking advantage of people or simply using them for their own purposes. In Chapter 3 I'll debunk that myth and provide you with a new paradigm for looking at relationships. You'll learn how to approach people as a generous relational investor instead of as a greedy transactional consumer. You'll take this generous relational mindset with you through the rest of the book.

- **Choose Your Own Adventure:** Use the self-assessment at the end of this introduction to help you discover the different types of relational investors that you need right now. The assessment creates a road map to guide you to the chapters you need to read first. Once you have the relational foundation of *intentionality* from Chapter 2 and *generosity* from Chapter 3, Chapters 4 through 9 will help you find the relational investors you need for your specific leadership challenges. Prioritize reading Chapters 1, 2, and 3 and then move through each chapter in order or read select chapters based on what you need right now from the self-assessment. You can even skim the Key Takeaways at the start of each chapter in less than two minutes. At the end of each chapter you will find reflection questions to help you turn the information in this book into personal insights. You will also find actions and experiments you can take to turn insights into action.

As you put intentionality behind your relational investors, you'll become a leader who lasts. You'll become a relational investor yourself. You'll build such strong social capital that you can generously reinvest your relational network in the growth and development of others by creating relational ecosystems.

The advice is simple, but it isn't easy: don't lead alone, build your trust circle. It's the relational secret to becoming a leader who lasts. This book will give you a blueprint to make it happen. Are you ready to get intentional about the relationships that will take you to the next level? Let's get started.

Take Action: Relational Investor Assessment

Directions: You need to be surrounded by a circle of relational investors to become a leader who lasts. As you consider this moment in your career as a leader, rate the extent to which you need each type of relational investor on a scale from 1 to 5. Add scores for each category as you go and enter them in the "Scoring Directions" at the end. Your scores on this assessment will show which relational investors are most important for you today and it will help you choose which chapters to prioritize reading first. Remember, while category is important, you need different kinds of relational investors, depending on the challenges you are facing in work or in the rest of your life.

Relational Investor Questions

1 = Not at All 2 = To a Small Extent 3 = To a Moderate Extent 4 = To a Great Extent
5 = To a Very Great Extent

STRETCH

Feedback (Chapter 4)

- I need relational investors who give me honest, challenging, yet caring feedback.   1   2   3   4   5

To be effective in my current leadership role and position myself for success, it's critical that . . .

- I increase my performance levels.   1   2   3   4   5
- I prevent leadership derailment.   1   2   3   4   5
- I discover my blind spots and areas for growth.   1   2   3   4   5

Add the scores:_____

Ideas (Chapter 5)

- I need relational investors who stimulate me to think in creative, innovative ways or to see things differently than before.   1   2   3   4   5

To be effective in my current leadership role and position myself for success, it's critical that . . .

- I generate novel, creative ideas.   1   2   3   4   5
- I initiate innovation and change.   1   2   3   4   5
- I challenge my assumptions about how the world works.   1   2   3   4   5

Add the scores:_____

Relational Investor Questions

1 = Not at All 2 = To a Small Extent 3 = To a Moderate Extent 4 = To a Great Extent
5 = To a Very Great Extent

Emotional Support (Chapter 6)

- I need relational investors who I would call if my life or career were crumbling. 1 2 3 4 5

To be effective in my current leadership role and position myself for success, it's critical that. . .

- I have friendship and comradery. 1 2 3 4 5
- I increase my satisfaction in life and in my overall career. 1 2 3 4 5
- I have people whom I can confide in when things are difficult. 1 2 3 4 5

Add the scores:____

Mentors (Chapter 7)

- I need relational investors who provide important guidance in my life and career. 1 2 3 4 5

To be effective in my current leadership role and position myself for success, it's critical that. . .

- I accelerate my learning and knowledge base. 1 2 3 4 5
- I have an example of how to lead well. 1 2 3 4 5
- I increase my job satisfaction and engagement at work. 1 2 3 4 5

Add the scores:____

(continued)

Relational Investor Questions

1 = Not at All 2 = To a Small Extent 3 = To a Moderate Extent 4 = To a Great Extent
5 = To a Very Great Extent

<table>
<tr><td rowspan="10">STRATEGY</td></tr>
</table>

Career Connections (Chapter 8)	• I need relational investors whom I will call tomorrow if I need to find a job.	1 2 3 4 5
	To be effective in my current leadership role and position myself for success, it's critical that. . .	
	• I have connections who can help me to find a new job or make a career change.	1 2 3 4 5
	• I stay aware of new opportunities that fit my skillset.	1 2 3 4 5
	• I keep a pulse on the competitive labor market.	1 2 3 4 5
	Add the scores: _____	
Advocates (Chapter 9)	• I need relational investors who would risk their reputation on my behalf.	1 2 3 4 5
	To be effective in my current leadership role and position myself for success, it's critical that. . .	
	• I advance my career and land a promotion.	1 2 3 4 5
	• I have access to key information, resources, or experiences.	1 2 3 4 5
	• I grow my influence and reputation.	1 2 3 4 5
	Add the scores: _____	

Scoring Directions:

Add up the items in each section on the previous page. Enter the numbers under "Your Score" and then circle the category where your scores fall. This will indicate strengths and gaps in your circle of relational investors.

High Need scores in a category indicate a type of relational investor that is especially important to your effectiveness as a leader right now. This is an area to pay critical attention to. Prioritize reading the corresponding chapters right away.

Medium Need scores indicate a potential vulnerability or an untapped strength in your circle of relational investors. Prioritize high need relational investors first and read the corresponding medium need chapters for further development when you are ready.

Low Need scores indicate an area of potential stability in your circle of relational investors. This is a category of relationships that you already have in place. Read the corresponding chapters to learn how you can build on that relational stability and continue to become a leader who lasts.

Relational Investors	Your Score	What It Means (Circle the category where your score falls)		
		Low Need	Medium Need	High Need
Feedback (Chapter 4)		4–8	8–16	16–20
Ideas (Chapter 5)		4–8	8–16	16–20
Emotional Support (Chapter 6)		4–8	8–16	16–20
Mentors (Chapter 7)		4–8	8–16	16–20
Career Connections (Chapter 8)		4–8	8–16	16–20
Advocates (Chapter 9)		4–8	8–16	16–20

Leaders Are Better Together

One of the greatest dangers in leadership is the level of isolation that can happen to a leader in the process of leading effectively. It's so pervasive that most leaders just learn to accept it as part of the job. If it's not addressed, however, it leads to burnout, breaking down, and acting out in harmful ways. Chapter 1 highlights the problem, the loneliness and isolation of leaders, and it provides a sobering view of the impact of leading without a circle of support. When you read this chapter, think about it like a check engine light that gives you an early warning before something breaks.

Chapter 2 moves from the problem to the solution, building your trust circle and establishing relational investors who help you lead at your best. We'll look at the three roles that the relational investors in your circle provide: stretch, support, and strategy. This sets up the architecture of the book and gives you a blueprint for building your circle, knowing that you'll have different people play different roles in your circle at different times. You'll discover how your circle of relational investors does more than help you avoid loneliness and isolation, it actually holds the key to high performance and lasting impact and legacy.

If lonely leadership is the problem, creating a rich trust circle should be the solution, right? Only if you build your circle the right way. Chapter 3 gives the secret ingredient to a healthy and sustainable trust circle—generosity. You'll learn how to invite other people to join your circle and invest in you in a way that's authentic, meaningful for them, and mutually beneficial. You'll also become inspired to consider how you can become a relational investor for other people, helping them build their own circle.

These chapters in Part I set the stage for unlocking the power of relationships throughout the rest of the book. Let's get ready!

1 | Leaders Shouldn't Be Lonely

Key Takeaways

- Leadership is lonely, but leaders don't need to be. Isolation and disconnection happen when you lead alone with no relational investors to show you your potential pitfalls or blind spots. Disconnected leaders can derail a company.
- Up to 67% of leaders derail or fail in their role and isolation is a key factor. These leadership failures cost organizations billions of dollars a year.
- The antidote to isolation and derailment is to become intentional about surrounding yourself with a circle of relational investors, your personal advisory board.
- Your trust circle helps you to become a leader who stands the test of time so that you can navigate critical transitions and serve others to your full capacity.
- To prepare for scale, sale, or succession you need relational investors who will stretch you to your next level, support you in your darkest hour, and strategically position you for success.

Leadership is lonely. When things go well in our work or our world, we sometimes give leaders more credit than they deserve. More often though, we don't give our best leaders enough appreciation or the support they need for the myriad of ways that they absorb our pain or create possibilities. Healthy leaders matter for families, workplaces, and communities. Leaders who stand the test of time realize and prioritize the need for meaningful, authentic relationships that stretch them, support them, and strategically position them. This social infrastructure is key to making leaders last. In this chapter, we'll talk about the importance of building your trust circle and how the right connections are the antidote to lonely leadership.

Social Infrastructure

In the Seattle area, where I grew up, it doesn't snow heavily very often. We're known more for rain and gray skies, but once every couple of years the region will get a few inches of snow, and the city slows to a halt. Schools and businesses will have later starting times until the snow melts, and then everything is back on track. But every 8–10 years Seattle gets a lot of snow, and the city is usually unprepared. The city shuts down due to the steep hills and the lack of snowplows and infrastructure designed for the occasion.

When this big snow comes, Seattle will occasionally lose power for a day or so. It's amazing what happens when the power goes out. After your batteries run out, you quickly realize just how much you rely on electricity. You can't hop online to check emails, post on social media, and depending on your appliances, you might not even have hot water or the ability to cook on your stovetop. In developed nations we take the incredible amount of infrastructure that moves life along for granted, until it suddenly turns off. In those moments, you can't help but recognize the networks that your life runs off, networks that you normally don't pay attention to: systems of power, plumbing and sewer, disposal of garbage and recycling, transit systems of highways and roads with public transportation. It's an ecosystem that you're largely unaware of in the background of life. The networks of relationships across our work and lives are similar in many ways. We take our social infrastructure for granted until we face the need to rely on them.

Without intentional relationships, we won't be able to serve others to our full capacity or navigate major business transitions smoothly. If there is one thing that can keep the metaphorical lights on and the water running for you as a leader, it's relationships with people who can surround you to stretch you, support you, and invest in you in strategic ways. The stakes are high and the need for support matters.

The Impossible Job of Leading

Can you imagine what it would be like if there was no one leading in the places you live and work? Leaders drive change and marshal people forward together to solve the most challenging problems in the world. You could be leading a business through a major organizational transformation to position for scale, sale, or succession or you could be running a nonprofit that's combating human trafficking in the slums. Every single one of those opportunities and challenges is fueled by the courageous efforts of leaders like you. Leaders who will undergo immense amounts of pressure, self-doubt, work–life balance issues, and innumerable highs and lows, to make each mission a reality. Your leadership makes your organization work.

In many workplaces, our expectations of leaders unintentionally set them up for failure. As a leader, people expect you to be a superhuman who will solve all their needs. People demand that you be hyper-connected and always available, yet they expect you to model work–life balance and effective time management. You are asked to be authentic and transparent, candidly sharing your struggles and fears but at the same time staying positive, inspiring, and composed in the middle of storms where the personal outcome for you is uncertain. Your team wants you to include people in decisions, while simultaneously being strong and decisive, casting and keeping a compelling vision without wavering back and forth. They want you to have bold convictions but at the same time they want you to be humble, willing to request and receive critical feedback. Leading is an impossible task. The act of leading is full of tensions.

It's time to revisit how you get the support you need. People are relational. We're designed for meaningful connections. Relationships are your social infrastructure. Leading is a high-stakes endeavor but, in most cases, leaders aren't equipped with the relational support they need to thrive and flourish for the long game. You need relational investors who stretch you to your next level, support you in your darkest hour, and strategically position you for success.

No matter your leadership level and role complexity or the context or industry, there is a critical need for you to surround yourself with a circle of intentional relationships, your own personal board of advisors. You need people around you whom you can trust. People who will both have your back and point out your blind spots. Leadership can be lonely, but leaders shouldn't be.

No One Leads Alone

Tina is a leader who understood the importance of relational investors. She was a rising executive in a global organization. She had a tremendous amount of responsibility and enjoyed her role overall, but she found herself being considered for a next-level opportunity as one of the top officers in the organization. This role would elevate her to an elite status and provide increased influence with some of the top leaders in the world across divergent disciplines. The role would also come with increased visibility to the media and public eye. It was a big role, and as she was preparing for her internal candidacy, I worked with her as a coach to thoughtfully craft her personal brand and position herself for the promotion.

One of the tactical items we worked on was her résumé. Résumés serve as a tool to narrate your career and tell the story of the value you bring. It's inspiring to hear the stories of people who have accomplished impressive feats, and she was a delight to speak with—a bold, confident, yet humble woman who inspired and empowered people with her presence. Tina's résumé was loaded with achievements and impact, but it was nearly impossible to work with her to position her personal brand.

The problem was that any time I tried to get her to tell me what she accomplished, she'd answer by describing the incredible team she had or a vendor who'd been an especially helpful partner or a mentor who had guided her wisely. Her inclusive approach was fine for the first few line items, but as we moved to her more impressive accomplishments, she kept pointing to the people around her. I started getting frustrated. "Tina, tell me what you actually did yourself. Having a great team and great partners across the business is fantastic, but none of them are interviewing for this role. We need to tell your story with your personal brand." Tina's response, with not even a twinge of frustration, caught me off guard: "I know that I need to share what my role in the projects was, but honestly, that's why it's so hard to write my résumé. When I look at anything meaningful that I've been a part of, the results are always due to a community of people around me. There's no way I could do any of those things on my own. I don't know anyone who does anything without other people."

Tina was right. No leader accomplishes anything meaningful in a vacuum. In fact, when you start to peel back the layers on any résumé line item, you quickly start to see that no one is a self-made leader. Even if you've had a challenging journey, at some point along the way, someone has invested in you, supported you, opened a door for you, or sacrificed for you. The whole story is that Tina was incredibly accomplished because she knew how to harness the energy of other people and how to build the right relationships around her. She accomplished more because of the people around her, and they didn't support her by accident.

Leaders Derail Without Support

Tina knew something that can take many of us a long time to realize—a successful life or career is enabled by the social infrastructure of relationships that we participate in. The reality is that the more responsibility or influence a leader has, the more isolated they often find themselves—even though higher stakes and complexity require greater support.

Behind every successful movement, initiative, product, organization, or family system are leaders who are stepping out and going first, catalyzing groups of people with vision or designing systems and processes that hopefully enable humans and communities to flourish. We need healthy sustainable leaders, and healthy leaders need relational investors.

Take the steep costs of executive derailment. Leadership researchers Joyce and Robert Hogan along with Robert Kaiser synthesized the research on leadership derailment and reported that between 30% to 67% of leaders fail in their role,[1] costing organizations billions of dollars a year.[2]

Take Alex Boyd, for example. Alex was facing a crisis. His energy consulting business had plateaued, and he was being weighed down with operational leadership that prevented him from strategic thinking and planning. Because Alex had filled many roles in the company, he'd developed a generalist skillset that was valuable because he could address varying needs, but dangerous because it kept him spread thin and unfocused on steering the direction of the company. He described how one day he realized that he was part of the problem, "I could do every job in the company—so I did. And that was the problem." He realized that he needed to restructure his team and allow his leaders to solve the operational problems in the business. He hired a COO and elevated his role to focus on the strategic thinking. As his time freed up, he confessed that he felt guilty for spending his time thinking instead of fighting fires. But he began to realize that this was how his leadership team could support him and how he could create space for them to run their business units most effectively. Today, his team pushes him to stay at the right altitude, and he was able to avoid a leadership career shipwreck. Now he has energy and focus to guide the business to the next level.

When you look at the top reasons that leaders derail or fail, relationships are always a major theme.[3] Not only are the financial implications staggering, but the impact on the people involved in an unsuccessful leadership transition can be debilitating. Failed leadership transitions erode the productivity and morale of the team who was caught up in the crash. The leader must now recover from a career setback or even a full-on derailment. Leadership failures have real implications.

This issue isn't unique to corporations and businesses. Even in higher education, an industry known for tenure and longevity, the average time in a university president role is only six and half years and decreasing,[4] and the average business school dean, a challenging mid-level executive role, is estimated to last only five years or less.[5] Leadership longevity is a problem in every industry. You need to be connected to relationships who are invested in keeping you on track.

The Isolation Trap

It's clear that we're hard-wired for connection.[6] Empirical research across psychology and the social sciences underscores Tina's experience in her life and work and yours too. Social support, in different forms, is a foundational part of healthy and happy living, from links to happiness and longevity, mental health, or even thriving for newborns and babies.[7] Leaders need connection. It's dangerous when leaders lead alone.

Isolation is the result of leading alone. An isolated leader is disconnected with no one to show them the potential pitfalls in front of them or to shed light on the blind spots around them. Being unaware of blind spots is a key reason that leaders derail.[8] If you have no one giving you candid, honest feedback, you'll never realize your fatal flaws till it's too late. Isolated leaders also carry the full weight of responsibility without anyone to shoulder their burdens. The weight of leading falls solely on them. At first, it's possible to hold up under the pressure but over time gravity usually wins and an isolated leader will be crushed. Isolation causes leaders to falsely believe that they have no one whom they can rely on for support. Isolation means leading alone.

At best, an isolated leader won't lead to their full potential, relying on their own capabilities and limited perspective.[9] Athletics provides a great example. In nearly every sporting activity, athletes train with other people so that they can go further, become faster, and get stronger. I've witnessed the same in leadership. Connected leaders refine each other. As the ancient proverb says, "iron sharpens iron." Think about a leader without mentors for perspective or advisors for input on important decisions. This leader will make decisions in a vacuum only to be surprised by the unintended results. Isolated leaders have fewer relational resources to draw on when making hiring decisions, forming partnerships, or taking big family risks like a major move or job change. Isolation is especially dangerous in critical transitions.

Isolated leaders are disconnected from reality. They find that their businesses don't carry the value that they believed. Lonely leaders don't keep pace with scaling, growing operations. The weight of their business demands starts to exceed their leadership capacity and strength. Many times, lonely leaders will hold onto their position too long because it defined their identity. These leaders avoid intentional succession planning because they can't picture life beyond their business.

At worst, an isolated leader can seriously hurt the people whom they are supposed to lead and even derail themselves. Think about the leadership scandals that hit the news: pastors, politicians, professors, and company presidents. The next time you see a leader who derails in some way, look for potential signs of isolation. While it's not the only factor, it's often a strong and contributing one.

Leaders who have people around them have built-in checks and balances, whether liked or not, to temper their thinking and question their decisions. These relationships can help leaders compensate for their weaknesses. Every leader needs people to care for them or counterbalance them. When you are surrounded by an intentional circle of relationships, it creates a safety net to catch you when you stumble. Better yet, it provides a personal board of advisors to perceive the peril ahead and navigate around it. Whoever is in your circle of relational investors, they can make the difference in your direction.

One example is Rich and Steve Gund, two brothers who forged a relationship that went beyond business and further than family. The Gund brothers took over a dysfunctional family business together. When they took over the business, the prior generation's relationships were toxic, and the business was stagnated. The brothers have complementary talents and different perspectives but a willingness to practice humility with each other. They realized that their ability to work together could be a difference maker. Rich describes himself as Mr. Inside, focused on operations and finance, with Steve taking on the role of Mr. Outside, focused on sales, marketing, and purchasing. From day one, they decided to align themselves on something bigger than themselves. They see the business as a vehicle for a life of purpose, not privilege, for themselves and their employees.

Together, they've relied on each other in an uncommon way. They work intentionally on their relationship, fine-tuning their trust in each other and allowing them to handle difficult family issues with dignity and respect. They've also intentionally been there for each other. Rich and Steve said, "When one of us gets tired, the other takes the baton and runs the next leg." They described their relationship as a healthy business marriage, a true partnership together in life and in work. The Gund brothers proved that isolation doesn't have to be the storyline and that connection is a powerful foundation for a leadership partnership.

So how does isolation happen? Some leaders purposefully isolate themselves to gain power or control. I've seen leaders intentionally design organizational systems that have fewer accountability mechanisms to challenge their vision or ideals. Isolation can be a choice, a protective mechanism so that they aren't challenged. Yet, most leaders don't set out to become isolated. Many lonely leaders slowly drift into isolation over time as they grow in responsibility.

The very nature of the role of leader is isolating.[10] It takes a great deal of intentionality and persistence to resist the fallacy of self-reliance. You are trusted with information that you must hold in solidarity, sometimes legally unable to share the burden that you are shouldering. Many leaders might not know who to trust. Does a team member genuinely want to help and assist you, or are they angling to position themselves for the next promotion? Which people on your team are smiling to your face and gossiping behind your back? Many leaders I've worked with desperately crave someone to talk to, but they don't know who or where to turn for advice or support or insight.

Other leaders want to grow and develop, but they don't receive enough quality feedback on how people perceive them. Criticism and complaints don't count. Awareness about the problems in the organization doesn't necessarily constitute as helpful feedback. When feedback is delivered, it's often met with skepticism. What are the motives of the person who shared the feedback? What's their agenda? It can be hard to filter what to heed and what to ignore. It takes intentional efforts to fight the inertia of isolation when you are leading.

Isolation isn't just a work issue. Countless leaders I've coached confess that the pressure of family obligations alongside a challenging job leave them feeling as though they have no place to get support. CEO owners often feel this the most. They feel personal responsibility for the business and the livelihood of their employees. The pressure can be overwhelming. Sometimes this gets exhibited in anger and impatience with their family members or in emotional distance to maintain the energy to survive another day. The ripple effects of isolation carry further than the workplace.

Unfortunately, isolated leaders are often the rule, not the exception. It's why I wrote this book. The antidote is the power of having the right relationships across the domains and seasons of life. The good news is that many leaders already have the relationships that they need—their circle is available, just not activated. Accessing those relationships is worth it.

A Road Map for Relationships

You don't need to lead by yourself. Surrounding yourself with the right people and becoming more intentional with the relationships you already have is a powerful way to increase your effectiveness now and for the long term. How do you get more intentional about surrounding yourself with the circle of relational investors you need?

In Chapter 2 we will learn about the architecture of an effective leadership circle, an intentional set of relationships that you can access for support, stretch, and strategy. Let's get intentional about getting connected.

Reflection Questions

- Leadership carries many expectations. What expectations do you have for yourself as a leader? What expectations do other people have for you? How do those expectations impact you, personally and professionally?
- What parts of your role as a leader cause you to drift toward isolation and loneliness? What structures in life keep you connected and protect you from drifting into isolation?
- Who are the most important relational investors in your life today? How does their support make you a better leader?

2 | Different People, Different Reasons, Different Seasons

Key Takeaways

- Your purpose will drive your circle of relational investors. Are you positioning yourself for scale and growth, for sale and exit, or preparing for succession?
- You need different people, for different reasons, in different seasons: stretch, support, or strategy. The key is the right people, for the right development, at the right time.
- Relationships that *stretch* you build leadership muscle, giving you the opportunity to challenge yourself and grow so that you have the capabilities you need.
- Relationships that *support* you develop leadership endurance, creating a buffer for stress and pressure, especially during critical transitions.
- Relationships for *strategy* create leadership agility, helping you capitalize on opportunities and create value.

Purpose and intentionality are a powerful combination for every area of life, especially our relationships. Making intentional efforts to become a leader who lasts creates a powerful buffer for the countless challenges that you will continue to face in your personal and professional life.

When you invite people to know you well and they invest in your growth, you can weather the storms of life and stay standing. That's because you have more to rely on than your own two feet—you can lean on whatever resources these people have that you lack. Meanwhile, these relational investors also see the strengths you have that they need, so they invite you to invest in them as well. Albert Bandura calls this pattern "agency by proxy."[1]

Decades of research is clear about the positive outcomes of an intentional circle of relational investors.[2] Creating this cadre of developmental relationships requires intentionality. When people have a developmental network in place, there are important links to well-being, lifespan and quality of life, career success, income, and a host of other positive results.[3]

Leaders in every context talk about the increasingly complex, ambiguous, and dynamic environments in which they lead. Every leader feels pressed for time. The pressure could be prioritizing competing projects, learning to delegate, or letting people go from your team. The good news, as we'll talk about in this chapter, is that it's possible to develop your capacity to handle challenges by tapping into the abilities and insights of others. The secret is having clear purpose for your network circle.

Relationships on Purpose

The most impactful circles of relational investors are driven by purpose. The purpose behind your circle will influence the decisions you make about the type of people you surround yourself with. Your purpose also drives the specific requests you make from the people you recruit to your trust circle.

When leaders recognize their need for relational investors, they become excited about building their network circle. They want to jump to the "how to" of their circle. Who should I reach out to tomorrow? What type of leaders do I need to learn from? What conversations should we have? Without a clear sense of the "why" behind your circle, the "what" or the people you enlist and the help you request will be vague. Don't waste anyone's time. Document the purpose for your circle at this moment, even if just a sentence or two. Specificity drives intentionality. This closes the gap between your desires and action. The stronger and more specific your purpose, the more likely you'll feel compelled to do something about it.[4]

If your purpose is meaningful for you and the people you serve, it will direct your relationship building efforts. Here is a list of examples of purposes that leaders have defined for their circle of relational investors:

- Improving delegation and time management to make room for planning and key initiatives.
- Generating ideas to innovate and keep an organization afloat during a major catastrophe.
- Learning how to manage growing family commitments alongside growing responsibility at work.
- Crafting an exit strategy and preparing your business for sale.
- Becoming a leader of leaders and working through other people.
- Learning how to live well and thrive through a difficult season of work.
- Managing the tension of being a parent who is present at home while succeeding as an entrepreneur in a growing business.
- Exploring the next steps in making a career shift or a role transition.
- Launching and learning how to sell a new product, program, or service that you don't have direct experience in.
- Relocating for work and struggling to help your family adjust to a new region.

- Becoming a manager for the first time and learning how to do it effectively.
- Creating a succession plan while planning for retirement.

Defining where you need people impacts how you rely on them. The people you identify as part of your circle will likely be honored and delighted to help you. Provide them with clear pathways to be of service and add value. This prevents your relational investors from feeling useless and will keep their investment strong over time. Clear agendas and specific asks energize your relational investors to serve you as you serve others.

Intentionality Versus Good Intentions

Purpose fuels intentionality. Intentionality drives the relationships you pursue, and it guides what you ask from them. Having a clear sense of where you are going and why helps you identify the relationships you need but it doesn't activate the power of those relationships. Purposeful circles of relational investors require intentionality. Intentional relationships are different from good intentions about relationships. Intentionality is about taking planned, measured actions in areas you can control or influence. Good intentions are desires, a good start but not enough to trigger behavior. Most people have good intentions, they just aren't intentional.

Many leaders rely on their available network versus an intentional circle of relational investors. Your available network is made up of people who are part of your natural network of relationships. These are people you've connected with over your career and life. Readily available relationships support you in seemingly serendipitous ways and are formed through the routine rhythms of life and work.

Think about the people that you rely on daily: co-workers, friends, or family. You don't need a lot of effort or intention to access these relationships. They often happen by proximity. On occasion these relationships provide intentional development, timely advice, point you toward a useful resource, or make a key introduction. There's tremendous value in organic relationships but it's likely that you aren't accessing the full potential of the wisdom that's ready for you. Depending on the overarching purpose that is driving you as a leader in this season, you probably need to access information or resources outside those circles.

Your circle of relational investors intentionally expands your reach. Some of the relationships in this circle might be part of your available network. Approaching these relational investors with intention can change the relationship. Many relationships in your circle represent people whom you don't connect with as part of your regular work.

Your intentional network is driven by your purpose in this season as a leader. They are people you've decided to make a deliberate effort to lean on. Sometimes you'll realize that you have a relational gap in your development. For example, when leaders map out their circle of relational investors, they often confess a lack of people who intentionally provide them with brutally honest, but caring feedback. Every leader has relational gaps. It highlights an area to be on the lookout for relational investors.

Getting intentional might mean a deeper conversation with the people whom you already know. You might ask a consultant who supports your team to share their perspective more regularly. I've been honored when clients consider me a key part of their circle of advisors. A long-time family friend could be tapped as a mentor. A CEO or owner whom you interact with at events in your industry could become an advocate for a big project. Other times you might keep watch for someone unexpected to come alongside you. The difference between your available network and your intentional network is planned, thoughtful efforts that lead to purposeful, mutually satisfying relationships.

Matching People with Purpose

We need different people, for different reasons, in different seasons. As you develop your circle with purpose and intentionality, consider enlisting relationships for stretch, support, or strategy. Some people will play a very specific role in your development for a specific time. Others may play several developmental roles across your work and life, both now and for the long term in the future.

Relationships That Stretch

Are leaders born or made? It's the nature versus nurture debate from my first Intro to Psychology class. The short answer is yes. Research in psychology has uncovered several personality traits that predict whether a person will either become a leader or be effective as a leader. For example, if you are more extroverted and open to experiencing new things, you are more likely to be asked to lead. If you are more extroverted and conscientious (driven and organized), then you are more likely to be effective as a leader.[5] Traits, or the "hard-wired" parts of who you are, account for between 30–50% of becoming or succeeding as a leader.[6]

But what if you are introverted and less open to experience? What if you have a lower level of drive? Good questions. Genetics and personality are important but that's not the whole story.[7] The experiences you have and the people who are around you matter too. The good news is that becoming a leader or succeeding as a leader is mostly linked to things beyond your genetics and your personality, between 50–70%! Challenging experiences build leadership. It's why relational investors who stretch you are important. Leadership is forged during crucible experiences, moments where you are stretched to the edge of yourself but not to the point of breaking.[8]

Think about your leadership capacity like your skeletal and muscular system. The size of your skeletal system is somewhat set. Bones can increase in density with diet and exercise, but at my age I won't be growing taller even if I take a lot of calcium and sleep well. Your muscular system is different. Diet, exercise, and sleep can dramatically impact your muscles, increasing the size, strength, or endurance you have. You can adapt your muscular system depending on your purpose, whether that be endurance training for a triathlon or maintaining a healthy lifestyle so you can play on the weekends. The good news is that your leadership capacity is just like your muscles. Your leadership muscles will grow if you work on them. You're not fixed by your genetics or personality.

The leadership gym where you can grow is all around you. If leadership is challenging, then welcome to the workout! Here are a few examples of stretching experiences that can grow you to the next level.[9]

- Leading in a role where things are growing in scope and scale
- Preparing your business for sale and planning your exit
- Taking a team or organization in a new direction
- Handling a turnaround situation
- Becoming a formal manager for the first time or becoming a leader of leaders
- Influencing others without formal authority
- Working with limited resources
- Dealing with a difficult personal situation alongside a demanding job

Experience is your classroom for development. Experts in the leadership development space refer to this with a short-hand moniker of 70-20-10 development.[10] This highlights that of the 50–70% of leadership development that isn't tied to genetic traits, at least 70% of that growth happens on the job (often more), during storms and challenges. The remaining 30% of that development happened through other people (20%), and through formal training environments (10%). Most of your development is happening through experiences. The same is true for your future successor. Don't just look for the person with the right stuff. Look for the person who is willing and ready to take on challenging experiences that build leadership muscle.

If leadership experiences are so important, why do we need relational investors to stretch us? The people who push you into challenging experience open the gate for the places where you will grow. The social capital you've accumulated over your career is the highway of opportunity for development. Relational investors who challenge you know that resistance is important for developing new leadership muscles. Relationships that stretch you give you the opportunities to challenge yourself and grow.

Two professors out of the University of Michigan showed why it's so important to have these sorts of people around you. Scott DeRue and Ned Wellman conducted a study that examined the extent to which leaders' skill development increased as they took on greater levels of pressure in a stretching experience. What they found is that when stretch and challenge increases, development and growth also continue to increase, to a point.

Even though stretch leads to growth, too much stretch can cause you to snap. The benefits of challenging experiences have a diminishing return. But they also tested ways to offset this diminishing return. One of the factors was the availability of feedback, from the job itself and from other people. Even though we know that stretching experiences help you grow, too much stretch will cause you to break, unless you are getting rich feedback and support throughout the process.[11]

What DeRue and Wellman found was like my experience in the weight room in high school and college. On my own, I quickly reached my "1-rep max," the capacity for how much weight I could lift. My strength plateaued. Then my best friend started joining me on a regular basis. He pushed me to add more weight to each workout. I knew that if my muscles failed that he was there to "spot" me and catch the weights, so I kept increasing the level of difficulty. He also challenged me, stretching me to "push one more time" or "add just a little bit more weight" on the bar. His partnership exponentially increased my strength and my 1-rep max doubled across every lift.

As you intentionally build your circle, recruit relational investors who help you to move beyond your comfort zone. Who will stretch you? Who will push or pull you into experiences that will propel you to the next level?

Relationships That Support

Challenging experiences are the classroom for leaders. Intentionally inviting relational investors to stretch you is necessary, but it isn't sufficient. You need people to stretch you and people to support you. Too much stretch without support will have a counterproductive effect. With the right amount of pressure your body develops strength but under too much pressure, muscles fail, and bones and ligaments can tear.

Every leader has a storm that is coming around the corner, the only question is when. One of the most powerful ways to create buffers for stress and pressure is to be surrounded by relationships you can retreat to for support. Who can you surround yourself with to get ready for the next storm? Who will stand by your side to help absorb the shock? Who are the people you can go to for advice and coaching? Who reminds you to focus on the things that are in your control? Who has an objective point of view that grounds you in reality?

Relational investors who bring support are often outside of your workplace. I was a researcher on a study that asked people whom they relied on during difficult times at work. Overwhelmingly, most people listed the names of family members, friends, or peers outside of their organization.[12] Whether at work or in your family, what matters most is knowing that you have the support you need when things get tough.

The relationships that stretch us build leadership strength and muscle. The relationships that support us develop leadership endurance. Some of the people you lean on will help to stretch you, others will support you, many will do both, playing multiple roles as investors in your development. If you have stretch and support in place, the third relational investor you need is strategy.

Relationships for Strategy

Strategic relationships are crucial to your ability to navigate leadership crucibles. These relational investors position you to make an impact. These people can open a door for you to walk though that was previously closed. Sometimes our strategic relationships go further by creating a door for us that we never knew existed. A strategic relationship can be someone inside your organization or a key external partner. Strategic relationships can connect you with the right client, help you find key talent to hire, or direct you to the person who will buy your business.

There are three common themes and one common misconception about strategic support. First, strategic relationships create opportunities or point us in the direction of opportunities. It's crucial for you to have people who advocate for you and create new opportunities. Second, strategic relationships bring insight or wisdom as you make important decisions. You might have too many decisions to make. The challenge becomes discerning which possible pathways you should take. Strategic relationships have unique knowledge, expert perspective, or wisdom to offer in high-stakes decisions. Third, strategic relationships position you to get ready for future opportunities. Like a chess master or the coach of a sporting team, strategic relationships see the big picture and can help you move forward with purpose.

Strategic relationships are indispensable but there is also a misconception. The fallacy about strategic relationships is that they are cold and calculated, perhaps even selfish. If your aim is to develop relationships that help you grow for the sake of others, then the people who depend on you need you to be strategic. Strategy is good if we're strategic in the right direction. We'll talk more about how to be intentional and strategic with the right motives in the next chapter. Strategic relationships can be mutually beneficial and even marked by generosity.

Relationships that stretch you build leadership muscle. Relationships that support you develop leadership endurance.

Relationships for strategy create leadership agility, helping you capitalize on opportunities.

Different People for Different Reasons in Different Seasons

Some leaders find mentoring relationships unfulfilling. They'll say that they didn't have chemistry with a mentor or that the person wasn't able to meet all their needs. Sometimes you might stumble upon a super relational investor who brings it all—stretch, support, and strategy—but this isn't the norm.

Building a diverse "personal board of advisors" is powerful for becoming a leader who stands the test of time. For years, social scientists have reported meaningful findings on the positive impact of mentors. In 2001, researchers Monica Higgins and Kathy Kram changed the game for mentoring. They created a new way to think about mentoring with the concept of a development network—a constellation of mentors.[13] Instead of one person, this freed people to think about the range of mentoring voices who provide different levels of value in different ways over different times. This new approach expanded the way researchers think about the people we need around us. Instead of finding one mentor when you are early in your career, we now tell people to find different mentors for different reasons and to look for relational investors throughout your career.

Today, many people call your development network your personal board of advisors. Corporations have advisory boards to steer their direction. Leaders can have personal advisory boards to steer their careers. Even if you have a formal board in your business, you still need a personal advisory board to cover the gaps. In this book I've been describing the people in your development network as relational investors. I use the terms development network, personal board of advisors, and your circle of relational investors synonymously through this book to describe the relational investors whom you intentionally rely on. If you are leading a pivotal transition, you need these people around you.

When it comes to relational investors, we need different people, for different reasons, in different seasons. The key becomes having the ability to connect with the right people, for the right development, at the right time. Some relationships will walk closely with us; others will be there for a particular season—perhaps serving a need for the moment and reappearing later or moving into a different role in our life over time.

Dr. Rob McKenna is an example of a relational investor who gave me the full package: stretch, support, and strategy. As my professor, he provided support as a mentoring voice, sharing advice and guidance on my future journey. He also brought me strategy by opening doors and opportunities that I hadn't considered. At one point he invited me to apply to join his PhD program, which transformed my career path. Years later, as a business partner he continued to stretch me and provide helpful feedback on my development as an executive. Dr. McKenna is an example of someone who was invested in me in many ways.

When a relational investor wears multiple hats in your growth, it's rich. Most of the time, though, a person will play one maybe two critical roles in your journey. It's rare to find a "hero" who covers most of your developmental needs. Even though Dr. McKenna played a powerful role in my career, he couldn't meet my every developmental need; no single person can.

Shift your perspective from looking for one mentor who covers all your bases to building a circle of relational investors. This frees you to move from relying on one person to develop you. Instead, build a board of advisors and access a richer base of diverse people who play important, but different roles in your life. You can still have meaningful mentors who make significant investments in you, but it takes the pressure off finding the "perfect" relational investor.

The idea of a circle of relational investors also takes the pressure off you as a leader with your own team. You can't provide for every development need for your direct reports. But you can help them create their own board of advisors that goes beyond you. This gives you permission to become a connector who finds people to support your team in ways that you can't. This is a great strategy for developing successors too. Help the leader behind you to build a strong personal advisory board and it will accelerate their development. They'll also bring wisdom and resources that you never imagined. You can't be everything to everybody so don't expect every relational investor to be everything for you. It can set you up for disappointment and it isn't fair to the person who is investing in you.

Perhaps the greatest honor I receive in my advisory work with leaders is when they share how empowered they are now that they have a partner in the growth of their business—they aren't alone. I know that I can play many different roles in their work and life and that my roles will evolve as our relationship develops. I don't have to meet all their needs, because I can't. I can bring in one of my partners to play a role that I can't or tap into my circle to support with a just-in-time need. Ultimately, if my clients feel connected, there is no limit to what they can accomplish. Kathy Thaut is one of those clients. As she looked at the last leg of her career, she wanted to grow the value of her plumbing business and honor the legacy of her late husband who she started the business with, but she didn't want to do it alone. Her trust in me and my partners and the resulting confidence she had to grow her business and build a future for her team when she had strategic support and insight was one of the greatest rewards in my work. Having traveling companions is invaluable for the journey of leadership.

Aligning Your Goals with Your Relationships

Who should you rely on and what do you need from each person? This goes back to intentionality. It depends on your goals and the outcomes you are looking for. It takes different networks to reach different goals.[14] That's why identifying the purpose behind your network is critical before you act.

It takes a different network to sharpen your ability to think in creative and innovative ways than it takes to open doors and position you to transition in your business. You might find that you've built a strong external network outside your organization, positioning you for your career transition. Perhaps you are a rising leader, and you haven't been as intentional about the internal network you need to create the opportunity for a promotion. We need different people for different reasons.

Relationships keep us on track as leaders and increase our effectiveness for the people we serve. But before we begin adding people to our circle, we must address the practice of networking itself. Some people love networking, some people hate it, but everyone has a mental picture of what it looks like and a gut reaction to it. In truth, many misunderstandings of networking float in leaders' minds—these will wreck our efforts to build an intentional circle of relational investors if we don't uncover them. We need to learn how to treat people as a treasure, not a transaction; how to love them, not leverage them. To build a network that sustains us for the long term, we need a different relationship paradigm. That's where we turn next.

Reflection Questions

- Describe the purpose behind the relationships in your circle of relational investors. Are you in a moment of scale, sale, or succession? Where do you need to grow as a leader to navigate that critical transition?
- Do you have a greater need from relational investors for stretch, support, or strategy? Why?
- Who is one person you could be more intentional about relying on during this current season in your life and leadership? What is the next conversation you can start with them?

Take Action: Relational Investor Map

1. What is the purpose behind your circle of relational investors? Why do you need relational investors right now?
   Write down your answer:

2. Fill in the table on the below with up to three names for each relational investor category. You can list a person in multiple categories.

3. On a scale from 1 to 10, rate how satisfied you are with the relational investment you are receiving from the relationships in each category.

Relational Investor Category	Names	Rate 1–10
Feedback		
Ideas		
Emotional Support		
Mentors		
Career Connections		
Advocates		

4. Fill in the radar graph to visualize the strength of your circle of relational investors.

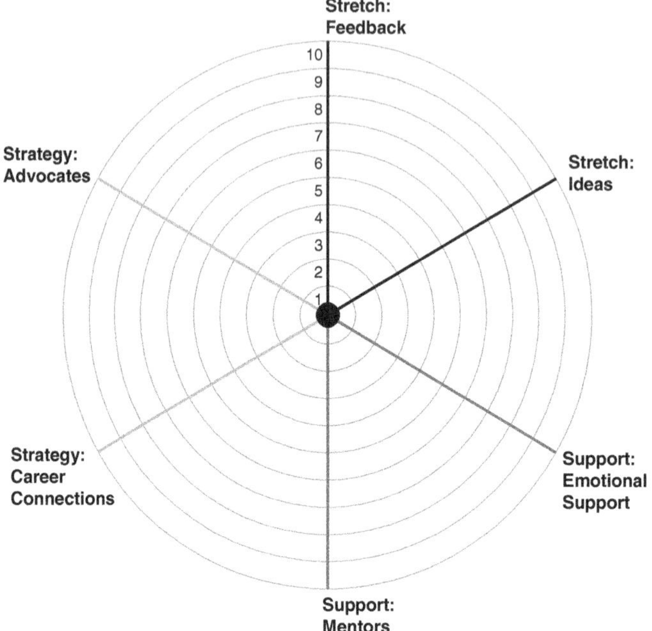

STRETCH

- **Feedback:** Relational investors who give you honest, challenging, yet caring feedback.
- **Ideas:** Relational investors who stimulate you to think in novel, innovative ways or to see things differently than before.

SUPPORT

- **Emotional Support:** Relational investors you would call if your life or career were crumbling.
- **Mentors:** Relational investors you go to for important guidance in your life and career.

STRATEGY

- **Career Connections:** Relational investors you would call tomorrow if you were looking for a job.
- **Advocates:** Relational investors who take a risk to put their reputation on the line on your behalf.

3 | Networking Doesn't Have to Feel Gross

Key Takeaways

- There is a dark side to intentional relationships. Intentionality with relational investors can become transactional and self-centered, making you a greedy transactional consumer of relationships.
- Relationships become meaningful when you shift your mindset from being a greedy transactional consumer to a generous relational investor.
- Generous relational investors ask a different question. Instead of starting with "What can I get?" they ask, "What can I give?"
- Generous relational investors believe that people aren't a process, people are the purpose.
- Generous relational investors get more than they give by giving more than they get.

Relationships matter for your development and sustainability. Being surrounded by people who bring stretch, support, and strategy sets you up to lead well for the long term. It also protects you from the dangers of isolation. Because relationships are so crucial, we know it's important to be intentional about them. But there is a dark side to intentional relationships. Becoming intentional about relational investors can easily become transactional and self-centered. The good news is that adopting the mindset of a generous relational investor will grow you as a leader and transform the way you approach relationships across your whole life, whether you are giving or receiving. This chapter is going to show you how.[1]

Knowing the Right People

In graduate school, there was a student I looked up to. His name was Peter. Peter was smart, articulate, and winsome. He was the type of person I wanted to be like. One day I saw Peter in the library. It was his final quarter in our program, and he was about to graduate. "Peter, you made it! You must be so excited!" His response surprised me, "Yes, but I haven't really built my network like I should have, so I don't have any jobs lined up yet." His answer terrified me. If someone as impressive as Peter did not have a job, then what chance did I have? As the son of two immigrants, education was the key to success. I could not afford to waste this opportunity. I left that conversation feeling anxious and fearful. I needed to find a way to protect my career. The stakes were too high for me to finish school without a job.

Then I remembered the advice I'd been given countless times. Go network. Build relationships. It's all about who you know, not what you know. They were right. Education wasn't the highway of opportunity; it was merely an on-ramp. The highway of opportunity is social capital. Your network. The people you know and more importantly the people who know you.

I was determined. Driven by fear, I set off to build a network that would guarantee my success. I spent as much time as I could building relationships with people who could hire me when I graduated. I made intentional efforts to join relevant professional associations. I secured mentors. I even assembled a "personal board of advisors" at the advice of a mentor. The process worked, but it didn't feel right.

I was meeting the right people. I was having meaningful conversations. Job opportunities started to open. My plan was on track. There was just one problem. Even though I made all the right moves it just didn't feel right. Networking and building relationships began to feel gross. I was approaching people as a transactional consumer, not as a relational investor. My driving question was focused on "What can I get from this person?" "How can they help me?" I was asking the wrong questions.

Networking Was a Necessary Evil

Networking had become a necessary evil. It felt gross. Then, one day the tables were turned. I saw a childhood acquaintance at a coffee shop. We started a conversation. He then spent the entire time trying to convince me to join the multi-level marketing scheme that he was a part of. You see, the more people he signed up underneath him, the more money he would make. But that's not all, he'd help me build an empire as well. In fact, he told me that I could make so much money that I'd never need to work again. I could provide for my parents as they aged. I could give back to them for all that they had given me. All by helping people change their spending habits to buy products from us. Products that they were "already going to buy anyways."

It felt like he was looking at me with cartoon dollar signs in his eyes, only focused on what he could get. How he could use me and leverage my relationships to build his little kingdom. I felt like I needed to take a hot shower afterward. It was at that moment that I began to realize, if networking and building relationships ever feels gross then you must be doing it wrong. There must be a better way than being the transactional consumer in relationships. "What can I get from you?" wasn't enough.

This approach to networking and relationship building was reinforced by a professional online social network that I was a member of. I received an email notification encouraging me to invite others to the platform. It read: "Add connections, build your empire, reap the rewards." This summed up the transactional mindset I was beginning to revolt against. When I read this for the first time, I wanted to throw up. Building professional relationships should never make you feel dirty.

It turns out that social scientists have studied what I experienced. In 2014, researchers from the University of Toronto, Harvard, and Northeastern teamed up to investigate the impact of building social networks on people's sense of morality.[2] They conducted four rigorous studies in laboratory and real-life settings. What they found across their work was that building relationships for selfish pursuits left people feeling "psychologically dirty" and even "morally stained." In fact, when people felt dirty after networking, they were even more likely to buy soap and shampoo. They literally wanted to wash themselves off!

Decades of research confirms the common advice about networking. Building social capital positively impacts all sorts of outcomes like job performance, promotions, salary levels, employability, and more.[3] If you want to build your career or your business, then networking is a good strategy. But here's the dilemma, when people feel dirty after networking, they make less efforts toward those relationships, even though those relationships were critical for their careers.[4]

There was a reason that I felt gross when I approached people as a transactional consumer instead of as a relationship investor.

Asking a New Question

How can you do relationships in a way that you don't feel like you need to rinse off after every coffee meeting? My mindset shifted. I started to see my relationship building activities as more than a means to secure my career. I started to ask a different question. Instead of, "What can I get from this person?" I began to ask, "What can I give to this person?" Everything changed. As my perspective started to shift, so did my attitude and experience. Building relationships was driven less by fear and more by joy. I began to have genuine excitement to hear a person's story, learn from them, and look for ways to serve them if possible.

Relationships that bring stretch, support, and strategy are critical for healthy leaders. If networking and relationship building has so many positive outcomes, how can you build a circle for your development and maintain your integrity in the process? Is it possible to build mutually beneficial relationships? Can the very act of connecting go beyond transactional and purely self-serving? What would change if you could build relationships marked by generosity, even if you were the one being invested in?

Generosity Beyond Reciprocity

I discovered generous relational investors who introduced me to a different paradigm. Jeff Rogers, a business owner in Seattle, was one of them. If you meet with him for coffee, you quickly realize that his goal is to learn how he can serve you, not how you can serve him. He'll carefully listen to what you are working toward and focus the conversation on ways he can be part of your success, often ending with a meaningful introduction to someone he knows. Jeff started a business that provides interim executive leaders to other businesses. In his business, results matter. But you'll never get the sense that he's looking to exploit you or get something one-sided from his relationship with you. Do Jeff's relational skills help drive his business forward? Absolutely, but if you ask him to share more about his approach, you'll discover that business outcomes aren't what drives him. His motivation is service. Adopting this new mindset moved me from being a greedy transactional consumer to a generous relational investor.

Relational investors leave people better than they found them. The focus is not on "giving to gain" or even about "paying it forward" so that positive things circle back around for you one day. Relational investors are focused on giving out of the overflow of who they are and what they have already been given. Relational investors bring generosity beyond reciprocity. They ask a different question. Instead of starting with, "What can I get?" they ask, "What can I give?"

Pathology or Potential?

What can I give to this person? The question represents a mindset shift from fixating on pathology to looking for potential. The human default is to focus on pathology.[5] Pathology is all about the things that are going wrong. The barriers, the obstacles, the brokenness. My PhD is in Industrial-Organizational Psychology. For decades, psychology—and many other human-centered disciplines—has focused on pathology. What's broken and how can we fix it? Over the last 40 years, there has been a revolution that pushed against pathology to look for potential.[6] What is going well? What is working? How do we make things even better? It's a shift from scarcity to abundance, an assumption that there is opportunity and potential to be realized.

Both are necessary. It's important to understand barriers and limitations but also to see possibility and potential. But our baseline is often self-preservation. How do I make sure I secure a job, protect my career, or position myself for success?

When I moved beyond my fear of finding a job, my perspective shifted from protecting my pathology to pushing for potential. As the old saying goes, "It's even better to give than it is to receive."

A Lifestyle of Relational Generosity

"I'd love to be generous, but I just don't have anything to give to others right now." I hear this a lot from leaders who want to give but don't feel like they have anything of value to reciprocate to their circle of relational investors. The idea of becoming a generous relational investor feels like a great aspiration but not a reality.

The good news is that you don't have to be in a position of wealth or power to become a relational investor. Remember, I was a poor graduate student. I discovered that generous relational investors give their time, treasure, and talent. Generosity looks different in different seasons. It could be as simple as the gift of your undivided attention, giving someone your full focus. It might be a heartfelt thank you note, showing gratitude toward a relational investor who brings you stretch, support, or strategy. Generosity can look like offering to help a co-worker who is behind on a deadline. You can also be generous with your relationships and offer someone a valuable introduction. You might realize that you can add value to two of your connections by introducing them to each other. You make the introduction without expecting anything in return. Generosity could even be as simple as the offer to review someone's résumé for them. The possibilities for generosity are only limited by your imagination. Becoming a relational investor is a choice. It's a lifestyle. It's a new way of being that reflects a new way of thinking.

In the psychological sciences, being a generous relational investor is also known as "prosocial motivation." Mark Bolino from the University of Oklahoma and Adam Grant from the University of Pennsylvania reviewed and summarized 25 years of research on prosocial motivation.[7] They defined it as simply "The desire to benefit others or expend effort out of concern for others." People who are higher on prosocial motivation are more likely to say that they want to help others in and through their work and that they draw energy from working on tasks or projects that can possibly help other people.

Generous relational investors believe that people aren't a process; people are the purpose. And business is all about people. The goal isn't to leverage relationships, or extract value from people. It's about building meaningful, generous, mutually beneficial relationships and focusing on how you can serve people, how you can give to them—even if they are helping you. You might not get anything back right away, or even at all. But there is still value in the relationship. Generous relational investors believe that every person has inherent dignity, value, and worth, regardless of the outcome.

Dr. Aaron Christopher, owner of Walla Walla Orthodontics, lives this out as he runs a thriving practice in an unconventional way. When you walk into one of his five offices you expect a cold and sterile dental clinic. Instead, you are surprised by colors and lights and life.

There's a slushie machine, party music, and staff who seem genuinely happy to be at work. Patients are even having fun and leaving with smiles—which ironically is the point of getting orthodontic work! If you pick any metrics of success in his industry, his team exceeds them. The feeling you get is contagious, but it goes deeper than just a vibe. Aaron has worked to make his values move off the walls and into the hearts of his people. It starts with Aaron's core belief that relationships are everything.

Aaron told me of a crucible moment that would define his conviction about relationships and culture. He was struggling through the demands of Harvard dental school and his father tragically died in a plane crash. Not long after, he and his wife lost one of their twins at birth. His life was rocked. He realized that you cannot cut yourself off from your tribe and expect to flourish. He turned to his family and close friends. Later, when he bought his clinic, he had a team of six staff and a toxic culture. He wanted to have a people-first practice, but his leadership skills were lacking, and he couldn't turn things around. Instead, half of his staff quit. He decided to try something different; he rebuilt his team by hiring for heart and training hands instead of hiring for skill and hoping for alignment. He went on a personal leadership development odyssey by reading as many books as he could, creating his own version of the discipline of dental school for the elusive skills of leading and building culture. He began to make his practice all about people. His company's purpose emerged as the following: "People deserve two things: to have fun and be loved." Everything changed. He decided to make his office feel like a home, not a clinic. He set out to create a completely different cultural experience for every one of his team members and his patients. The practice grew dramatically and the cultural architecture he created transferred to every new location he opened. Discovering that people are the purpose turned Aaron into a relational investor who now lives to pour into people. Today, he sees leadership and culture, investing in people, as the most important part of his job.

Giving and Receiving

When I talk about becoming a generous relational investor, sometimes people think that I'm telling them that they should only give, and never receive. This couldn't be further from the truth. One leader recently told me, "Even when I'm focused on serving in a relationship, I still know that there's something transactional that I need to get to at some point." Generous relational investors know the value of both giving and receiving.[8] Prosocial motivation is different from purely selfless altruism and different than self-serving greed.[9] You can be fully engaged in serving others and at the same time still aware of the practical needs you have. Allowing someone else to invest in you is a gift to them. The ultimate relational investors know how to give and receive.

What does giving and receiving look like as a leader? You are tasked with getting things done with and through other people. That's your job. When you ask a peer or a team member to help you accomplish your goals you do so with awareness of your needs. If you didn't have a need, you wouldn't be initiating the conversation in the first place. You need the person to help you get something done. That's clear to you and to them. At the same time, just because you have a request doesn't mean that you can't be equally focused on the other person. You can care for them as you work with them to achieve results that you need. You can consider your own needs and consider the needs of the other person. Giving and receiving are not mutually exclusive. Becoming a generous relational investor is about looking out for the interests of others, even when there is something you need to accomplish. It's holding both together, your needs and their needs. That paradox makes sense in practice.

Consider these two examples. Think about a relationship where you are meeting to sell a product or raise funds for a project. When you meet with a potential client or donor you have a clear objective for the meeting and it's no secret. If you have the mindset of a generous relational investor, you will look for a way to serve the potential client, regardless of the outcome of the meeting. Even if you can't discover a tangible way to serve them, your attitude and affect will change the nature of the relationship. This doesn't change the purpose of the meeting, but it does keep the door open for genuine care for the other person. This type of approach doesn't leave you feeling dirty or guilty because you are aligning your personal needs with the other person. You refuse to get what you want at the expense of someone else's well-being. This authentic approach leads to deeper trust over time.

Imagine if your relationship building efforts weren't hindered by guilt or a dirty feeling. Relational investors build networks to give and serve, even when they are on the receiving end. This freedom gives you the willingness to ask for help when you need it. You can't lead alone for the long term. The most generous relational investors are the ones who are most aware of what they've received from other people. They give from a place of abundance.

Investing for the Long Term

Years after my pivotal conversation with Peter in the library, I found myself back in a university, helping lead a graduate business program. I was meeting a potential student for my program to learn about his goals for the future. He was a great candidate and I really wanted him in my program. But over the course of the conversation, I realized that what I had to offer wasn't the best fit for him. Reluctantly, I pointed him in a different direction. A year later, I had another similar conversation with a young woman who was also exploring our program. She was amazing. Her goals aligned with our training, and she became one of our best students. It wasn't till after she started when I discovered that she found out about our program from the young man I'd met with over a year before. He told her that if she met with me, I'd put her interests first and that if she wasn't a fit that I'd point her in the right direction. Focusing on the interests of other people can pay off over the long term, but that's not the point. There is nothing more rewarding than giving to other people. Oh, and by the way, my classmate Peter ended up getting a job after graduation too.

Cultivating Your Network

My parents certainly impressed the value of education on me, but they also demonstrated the value of generosity. They have been avid suburban gardeners for more than 40 years. They have been composting before it was the cool thing to do in Seattle. Every year they carefully till their soil, fertilize it, prepare seeds, plant, water, and care for their garden with great intention. As time goes on, different plants will blossom and produce fruit at different times. They tend their garden well. Every year they harvest so much produce that there is absolutely no way that they can possibly eat it all. They have so much that it will spoil, it will go to waste. What do they do? Instead of letting it spoil, they spoil their friends. They take all the excess, they put it in bags and baskets, and they generously share it with their friends and neighbors! Often, they even use their extra seeds to help friends start their own gardens.

As I look back, I realize that my parents didn't garden just for themselves. They certainly enjoyed the fresh fruits and vegetables, but they had equal if not greater joy in giving to the people around them. The relationships in their lives represented a place for giving, not a vehicle for getting. My parents demonstrated that you get more than you give by giving more than you get. Our networks of relationships are also like a garden. If we tend our circle of relational investors well it will grow and produce fruit. So much in fact, that there is no way that we can consume it all ourselves. We can share those relationships with someone else who needs what that person has to offer. When we give relational capital, we don't lose it. It doesn't decrease; it increases. We can even help someone start their own garden.

Moving from being a greedy transactional consumer to a generous relational investor is rewarding. It makes work human and meaningful. But there is a potential dark side to generosity too.

Avoiding the Dark Side

Every strength or virtue has a corresponding weakness, often depending on the context. In the same way, focusing on generous, authentic relationships isn't without challenges. Not everyone is motivated by service to others. Some people don't feel dirty when they use other people.[10] Other leaders work hard to appear selfless but mostly to be well thought of by other people. But true motivations often become clear over time, especially if the person is just trying to get noticed or manage impressions.

Blaine, a mid-level executive, would often offer resources or connections to the people he worked with. On the surface it appeared genuine but over time his peers and direct reports came to realize that accepting help from Blaine meant that you owed him by putting yourself in his debt. He would make "deposits" in the relational bank account, and you never knew when the withdrawal would come or what it would look like.

Moving from the mindset of a transactional consumer to a relational investor is where it starts. But there are two common pitfalls that even the most generous relational investors experience: overextending yourself and slipping into selfishness.[11] Understanding these traps helps us avoid them and continue to keep our motivation to serve others strong.

Pitfall #1: Overextending Yourself

If you have a high desire to serve others, then one of the most common traps is the risk of overextending yourself and trying to be everything for everyone. The desire to serve and help people is different from the actual ability to meet the needs of every person we are in relationship with. There is a subtle difference between *caring about* people and *caring for* people. We all have a great capacity to *care about* many people, but we have a limited capacity to directly *care for* people. There is a difference between focusing on serving other people and focusing on being liked by other people.

Relational investors who last know how to accept help and to recognize their own limitations. My business partner, Alan Andersen, often reminds me that every person only has 168 hours in their week, no more and no less. Time is an equalizer. We all have relational boundary conditions that we can't reach beyond. Our limits keep us humble and force us to focus our efforts on who we directly care for.

Being mindful of personal limits allows a healthy leader to continue to invest in others and serve for the long term. This goes back to the importance of having a clearly identified purpose that we discovered in Chapter 2. Having greater clarity about your purpose and direction can help you discern when and who to say yes to and when and who to say no to. Relationships marked by purpose and intentionality allow leaders to develop the relational wisdom to know who to serve.

John found himself in a tough spot that challenged his priorities. He was a senior director in a highly visible, externally facing role. His job was demanding and he had meaningful commitments in the community alongside raising a young family. He didn't have the time in this season of life to connect with other people as often as he'd like. John had a heart for relationships and wanted to serve others when someone made an introduction to him. Wisely, John carefully considered his availability. When the opportunity to connect with someone came his way he'd stop and evaluate whether he was the right and best person to serve them. Often, he'd find someone else who was better aligned to meet their needs. John made a lot of thoughtful introductions and took fewer meetings. This practice helped John to prioritize his limited time till his capacity for meetings opened. He recognized his limits and found a way to maintain the posture of generosity.

Realize your limits and embrace them. This will help you develop the wisdom to know who to focus your relational investments in. The goal is to serve well for a long time. The best relational investors know when to say no.

Pitfall #2: Slipping into Selfishness

The first risk that relational investors face is overextending themselves and failing to recognize their limits. The danger is being generous to the point where they have nothing to give. On the other side there is a different pitfall. The second risk is drifting from generosity and slipping into selfishness. It's easy to lose sight of the inherent value of relationships and slowly begin to move from relational to transactional. If you have a demanding job, the need to achieve results can pressure you into making relationships merely a means to an end. This can be especially true when you are planning your exit strategy and tempted to be focused only on the business transaction ahead of you.

This pitfall is part of the human experience. I've found that even the most selfless person will realize moments when they've slipped into a self-centered approach to relationships. The leaders whom I've most admired are the ones who have learned how to take responsibility for their mistakes and then work to repair relationships that need mending.

Ash, a senior marketing executive, shared a story about when he left an institution that he'd invested over a decade of service in. He'd made many personal sacrifices because he believed in the mission. After a new CEO joined the organization, Ash sensed that there wasn't strong alignment anymore. He started to consider what a transition might look like. Before he started planning in earnest, an opportunity was presented to him. It was a great fit for the next chapter of his career and the stage of his family's life. When he made the announcement that he was leaving his role, he was shocked to receive harsh feedback from his peers and the CEO on his departure. Rumors had been spread that he was abandoning the mission and leaving them in a lurch.

Ash felt burned by his former friends. He was surprised when two years later he received a call from the CEO he'd left. They met and his former boss apologized for the way Ash was treated on the way out. He explained how he'd recently fired two caustic individuals who'd not only spread the rumors about Ash in the past, but who were continuing to display behaviors that harmed the progress of the organization. Ash was shocked but grateful that this CEO had the humility to follow up two years later to correct his mistake and apologize for how Ash had been slandered. This courageous act from his former boss opened opportunities for Ash to reconnect with old friends and colleagues.

Taking personal responsibility is hard but it's a skill that is worth working on. Mending relationships is often necessary. Personally, I've had to repair relationships many times. Several years ago, I was in a new role, leading a project with a tight deadline and high levels of visibility. The stakes were high, and I wanted to get my first big win with my new team. After leading a team meeting, one of the leaders I was partnering with approached me. He let me know that I was being selfish in my approach to running the project and that the decisions I was making to keep the project on time were negatively impacting others. It's never fun to hear that feedback but I was so grateful for the opportunity to repair the relationship with him and the rest of the team. Over time my ability to have those difficult conversations has grown as well.

Aaron Christopher, the culture-first owner of Walla Walla Orthodontics, described a phrase he uses with his family and his team, "Let's start over." When things go sideways, it's a watch phrase that signals the desire to get it right, extend and receive grace, and try again. He's even institutionalized corporate "Let's start over" off-sites if the team is drifting from their commitments to each other. He leads the effort and acknowledges where he's falling short and missing the mark and recommits to his team. It goes something like this: "I wrote down everything where I fell short and asked, 'Will you let me start over?'" Aaron leads by example and invites the rest of the team to ask the same. Facilitated carefully, it's a powerful culture recalibration and trust building exercise that keeps Aaron and his team members focused on each other and their patients.

It's easy to slip into selfishness, even if you started with a positive intent. The good news is that many relationships can be mended. Becoming a generous relational investor is about movement in the right direction, not about perfection. You can take responsibility when you've slipped into selfishness and get back to serving other people.

It's All About Relationships

Building relationships has challenges and it takes work, even when your motivations are to serve. Relational investors build generous, generative relationships by training themselves to ask, "What can I give?" instead of, "What can I get?" The long-term benefit of healthy relationships is worth the effort. Changing your mindset transforms your relationships and infuses meaning into your work. A generous mindset deepens your fulfillment, especially in relationships where you are giving or receiving stretch, support, or strategy. Most importantly, it helps you become the type of relational investor for other people that you want to find for yourself.

Becoming a generous relational investor starts with a new mindset, a different paradigm of relationships. What's your relational posture? Are you a greedy transactional consumer or a generous relational investor? Are you protecting your pathology or pushing for potential? As you surround yourself with a circle of relational investors for stretch, support, and strategy, remember to ask a different question and keep looking for "What can I give?" instead of "What can I get?"

Reflection Questions

- How would you describe your default approach to relationships? How is that similar or different to the approach that this chapter outlines?
- What would change if you started to look for creative ways to serve the people in your network?
- What would motivate you to become more generous and thoughtful with the relationships in your work and life?
- Make a list of ways that you can practically serve and care for the people in your network.
- Think of one relationship where you might be focused on getting more than you are focused on giving. What is one action you can take to proactively serve that person for their sake, not yours?

Take Action: Transactional Consumer Versus Relational Investor

Do you have the posture of a transactional consumer or of a relational investor? In each of the following 10 pairs of statements, circle the statement that most closely reflects your attitude or actions over the last 6 months.

- If you circle more statements on the left column than on the right, you might have the posture of a transactional consumer. The good news is that you can change this mindset. Read this chapter again before moving forward in the book.
- If you circle more statements on the right column than on the left, you might have the posture of a relational investor. Consider what you can do to continue to keep your motivation to serve strong.

Transactional Consumer	Relational Investor
• What can I get from this person?	• What can I give to this person?
• What's in it for me?	• How can I serve you?
• Focused on self over others	• Focused on both self and others
• Preoccupied by short-term gains	• Committed to long-term sustainability
• Seeing people as a "means" to an "end"	• Seeing people as the primary purpose
• Giving in order to gain at a later time	• Giving without expectations of return
• Valuing a relationship based on potential outcomes	• Valuing people based on their inherent dignity and worth
• Protecting my scarce opportunities	• Offering my abundant resources
• Motivated by fear	• Motivated by service
• Hoarding social capital and "key" contacts	• Sharing social capital and making introductions

Stretch

In every leadership book, coaching session, or training program, the importance of self-awareness is highlighted at some point. Self-awareness is critical for leaders, but it can easily become passé after you hear it again and again. Self-awareness is important because a leader who isn't self-aware—a leader who is unexamined—becomes a danger to others and even to themselves.

Unexamined leaders do not know how their presence is impacting others around them, positively or negatively. An unexamined leader doesn't realize how an overused strength can be a double-edged sword. Think about a leader whose strength is empathy and listening. That leader makes people feel seen and heard and valued. The same leader might unintentionally hurt people in their organization in moments when the greatest need is clarity and decisiveness, not consideration or care.

Unexamined leaders are simply bumbling around, accidentally doing some things right, but often causing damage without the awareness of their attitudes or actions. Growing in self-awareness is the result of deliberate, continual self-examination and self-definition—usually with the help of other people. The examined leader has taken the time to understand what they are like and how their actions impact other people.

Examining yourself with the help of other people focuses on your behavior, but it also includes what you think and what you feel. The interior life of a leader will always permeate the whole life of a leader. Attitudes and beliefs show up in behaviors, which, in turn reinforce attitudes and beliefs. Understanding your behavior, and the source of your behavior, allows you to course correct and avoid pitfalls.

Relational investors who stretch you are a necessary ingredient for examining yourself, increasing your self-awareness, and allowing you to see how you relate to others more clearly. Relational investors who stretch you increase your *intrapersonal* awareness, looking inside yourself, and *interpersonal* awareness, looking at yourself in relationship to others. Investing in relationships that stretch will be like receiving a new set of glasses or cleaning the windshield of a car. Suddenly, opportunities and challenges become clearer.

In this part, we will focus on two relational investors that stretch us. In Chapter 4, we'll look at relational investors who give you honest, yet challenging, feedback. In Chapter 5 we'll look at relational investors who stimulate new ideas and challenge you to think in creative, innovative ways or to see things differently than before.

Relational investors who give you feedback fill in the gaps between your limited self-understanding and reality. Investing in a feedback network can make the difference between derailing as a leader and growing as a leader. Increasing levels of responsibility correspond with increasing isolation and decreasing levels of helpful feedback—a recipe for leadership catastrophe. In Chapter 4, you'll learn how to set yourself up to receive regular, meaningful feedback and how to discern what feedback to act on and what to let go of.

Relational investors who challenge your perspective stretch you by expanding your imagination and provoking you to see the world in different ways. These relationships open possibilities and trigger your creativity and nimbleness as a leader. In Chapter 5, you'll learn the surprising benefits of regularly surrounding yourself with divergent thinking to help you navigate the complexities of leading in a dynamic world.

Building leadership muscle requires that we expand our capacity and invite relational investors into our journey who are willing to push and pull us to the next level as well. Let's get surrounded by people who stretch us.

4 | Feedback: The Feedback Filter

Key Takeaways

- Getting the right feedback will block or unlock your ability to successfully navigate scale, sale, or succession. Leading for the long term requires you to learn things about yourself that are important to change, but difficult to look at in the mirror.
- Getting meaningful feedback at the right time can be the difference maker for your success or failure. Feedback allows you to learn and even increase performance as the pressure rises.
- Feedback is usually the most underdeveloped part of a trust circle. The more responsibility you have, the less likely you are to receive helpful performance feedback.
- 33% of the time receiving feedback hurts performance more than it helps it. Asking for feedback is crucial for leaders but not all feedback has equal value.
- Filter the feedback you receive to determine if you need to (a) increase your performance, (b) lower your performance expectations, or (c) ignore the feedback.

We've all had a moment when we discovered spinach in our teeth, only to wish that someone had been caring enough to let us know. Honest, challenging, yet caring feedback is like staring in a mirror and getting a clear picture of how you look. Relational investors who stretch you with feedback are a key to becoming a leader who stands the test of time.

Feedback is especially critical during the crucible moments that leaders face. Preparing for scale, sale, or succession creates high-pressure moments that have the potential to refine you in the fire or just burn you. In Chapter 2 we saw that challenging experiences develop leadership muscle, up until a point. If you take on too much stretch, you'll break, unless you get regular feedback. Feedback allows leaders to learn and even increase performance as the pressure rises.[1] Getting meaningful feedback at the right time can be the difference maker for your success or failure. In this chapter, we'll look at the difference between feedback that helps and feedback that hurts. We'll also identify the actions you can take to get the right feedback, from the right people, at the right time.

The Emperor Has No Clothes

Children love to hear the story of the emperor who discovered that he had no clothes. The fable is so whimsical that even adults laugh. We imagine the emperor who is led to believe that he is wearing fine garments while his subjects continue to affirm him, fearful of sharing the truth. It's not until a young boy, unaware of social norms, breaks the news to the emperor that the truth starts to sink in. Like the emperor, you have blind spots that you aren't aware of till someone surprises you. If you don't have people who stretch you by giving you feedback, you increase your risk for derailing as a leader.[2]

I was the emperor early in my marriage. We were trying to find a tenant to take over our lease in the basement unit that we rented. We'd made a deal with our landlord that we could break our lease without penalty if we found someone else to take over our payments. The unit was a great find, especially for the location and price point.

Two friends who were about to get married had heard about our upcoming move. They came over one night to look at the unit. I was excited to showcase our home. My wife is a gifted artist and she'd done some great work with the interior. I was confident that our unit was the perfect fit for this couple. When they arrived, I made sure to show them all the amenities. This unit was a great value, so I wanted to make sure we didn't miss anything.

As soon as they left, I turned to my wife, Kristin, with excitement, "I think they loved the place; they're definitely going to take it. What do you think?" Her response shocked me, "Well, you did show them every flaw, blemish, and problem in the unit. I'm not sure I'd want to live here if I were them." Kristin graciously explained how I had showcased the loose tiles on the counter and how I ensured that they knew all the access points for spiders in the laundry room crawl space. I even made sure to tell them about the noise from our landlord upstairs when he played guitar for his girlfriend over the phone. She shared a long list of problems I'd pointed out. I started to realize how much of a mess I'd made as a tour guide. "I guess you're right. I wanted to show them how great the place was, but I pointed out all the issues instead." This story highlights how feedback closes the gap between actions and intent. My intentions had been good, but I had no idea how I was being perceived by others. Over the years I've been so grateful for people in my circle, like my wife, who give me honest feedback on how I'm showing up and how I'm seen by others. Oh, and no, they didn't rent the house. They found one with less features and benefits!

Feedback Is Critical for Leaders

Without feedback, your positive intent can have negative impact. You need people in your circle of relational investors who deliver honest feedback. It's funny to think of the emperor without any clothes or my embarrassing apartment tour, but those are low-stakes examples that make for great stories. When the stakes get higher the importance of feedback rises.

Feedback is usually the most underdeveloped part of a trust circle of relational investors. The more responsibility you have, the less likely you are to receive helpful performance feedback. If you own the business, you may get even less. Increased responsibility usually means decreased feedback.

Carl was an example of a feedback failure. He was a brisk, hard-driving leader known for getting results. He took over the company on the heels of a highly successful and well-loved leader. Carl's predecessor had guided a compelling, shared vision. She was respected by her team as a compassionate leader who listened carefully and led strongly.

Within a few weeks it was evident that Carl's style didn't quite fit the collaborative, consensus-focused culture he'd found himself in. The rifts with his team deepened. He informed his team that he cherished their feedback as he adjusted to his new role. Several team members carefully approached him to provide direct feedback on the impact of his actions. Despite what sounded like genuine requests for feedback, Carl never followed through to meet with his team members to hear their input. After several unsuccessful attempts, no one on his team took him up on future feedback requests.

Opportunities for minor corrective feedback snowballed into complaints to the board. Eventually an "anonymous 360 feedback survey" was sent out to gather input for Carl's performance review. Finally, Carl's team had an opportunity to formally share their grievances. Shortly after this survey was completed, Carl resigned from his role. It became clear that the emperor had no clothes. His perceptions of his performance didn't match with what others observed.[3] Taking initiative to seek feedback from relational investors is critical for your growth and performance.

The Right Feedback at the Right Time

Asking for feedback is crucial for leaders. But not all feedback has equal value. Researchers Avraham Kluger and Angelo DeNisi discovered surprising insights on the feedback when they conducted a large-scale summary of the most rigorous research on feedback.[4] One of the startling findings was that while feedback does increase performance, overall, the results were inconsistent. It turned out that about one third of the time, receiving feedback decreased performance instead of increasing it.

Just asking for feedback doesn't mean that the feedback you receive will help you grow. If you want to become a leader who lasts, you need the right feedback from the right people at the right time. How do you get quality feedback that increases your performance instead of eroding it?

Carl's story of a feedback failure is an all too common, sobering example of the impact of receiving feedback too little or too late. Early, quality feedback could have changed Carl's trajectory.[5] Carl was a talented leader, but he was isolated and disconnected with reality. He was leading alone but didn't need to be. He eventually transitioned to a great role where he was successful, but it took him time to find his next move. It also took his former team several years to realign several key initiatives and get the performance of the organization back on track. Carl's derailment could have been prevented, saving Carl and his team a lot of heartache and productivity.

We know that feedback is important. So how do you get feedback that increases performance and confidence, instead of eroding it? Let's break down the anatomy of feedback. We'll start by separately considering the differences between requesting feedback and receiving feedback, both positive and corrective. All feedback is constructive as it has the potential to build up the person on the receiving end. Some constructive feedback is positive and reinforces the things you are doing well and should persist in. Some constructive feedback is corrective, helping you adjust your course and close the gap between your actual performance and your ideal performance.[6]

The way you request feedback and the way you receive feedback also sets the tone for the people you lead. Will you help people feel comfortable bringing forward praise and critique? To receive a steady flow of helpful, healthy feedback, start by asking yourself two questions: (1) How do I request feedback, am I approachable? and (2) How do I receive feedback, am I coachable?

Requesting Feedback: Are You Approachable?

Even though Carl said he wanted feedback, he didn't create the conditions that made it easy to approach him. His lack of response and defensive posture kept his team from bringing forward the truth about his actions. This self-protection ultimately cost him his job. It also drained the morale of this team. If you are approachable, you will receive meaningful regular feedback that you can act on. Your team will stop delivering feedback to you if they sense that you really don't want it. Here are four ways to work on becoming more approachable and increasing the quality of the feedback you receive: ask immediately, ask for specifics, ask "What went well?", and ask the right people.

Ask Immediately

Corrective feedback is like a jug of milk; there's an expiration date for when it begins to spoil. The closer that feedback is to the event, the more likely you'll learn from it. The longer it takes to deliver corrective feedback, the weaker the impact.[7] If someone approaches you with feedback about your behavior from months ago, the details will be fuzzier in your mind. You'll be less likely to connect the dots between your intent, your behavior, and your impact. Even if you agree and thank the deliverer for the feedback, it won't form quite as strong of a connection in your mind. When you encounter your next high-pressure moment, be sure to solicit feedback from others as soon as possible if you want to learn from the event. The best feedback reduces uncertainty and increases clarity. Feedback that's close to the event will likely have more details and give you a clearer sense of what really happened.

Corrective feedback is even more helpful if you can see how you've improved over time. If you receive recurring feedback on a particular issue, stop and ask how your behaviors have changed over time. Seeing a positive trajectory motivates us to continue, even if we were given some hard truths to swallow.[8]

Asking for regular, immediate feedback is critical as a leader. It's also a powerful way to model a climate where feedback is natural and desired—where giving and receiving feedback is expected.[9] When you show the humility to learn and change it invites your team to do the same. Your courage gives others the unspoken permission to seek out feedback on their own performance. Be careful though, if you ask for feedback often but don't work on incorporating it, you can send a counterproductive signal about feedback. Don't ask for feedback unless you are ready to do something about it.

Ask for Specifics

How would you react if you were told that you're simply not a good leader? You'd probably want to gather more details to understand what that means. Vague feedback hurts more than it helps. Generalized statements give too much room for misinterpretation and not enough specificity for you to act on. Vague feedback bruises your ego without providing a pathway forward. Getting regular feedback is important, but specificity allows you to act.[10] Ask probing questions when you receive feedback. Your questions will draw out the nuance in a situation and help you set goals to improve.

When you make vague, lazy requests for feedback you'll receive vague, lazy responses.[11] Asking "What did you think about that board meeting?" is likely to evoke a parallel response, "I think it was good, you?" The more specific you can be when you request feedback, the more likely you'll get specific details. "When I challenged Sydney about the three-year plan in that meeting, did I come across as controlling and inflexible? I'm really trying to work on how I disagree but preserve relationships in the process." "Thanks for asking. I know you had good intentions, but your response did feel emotionally reactive. It seemed like all she heard was your tone, not your points. I think she might have taken your comments personally."

Specific, thoughtful requests are more likely to evoke thoughtful, helpful insights. Vague feedback doesn't give you anything to hold onto and can make any proposed change feel like something outside of your control. Specifics begin to help you see that you can change—even in small ways, that there is value in making a change, and that the impact of that change will have a positive impact that benefits you and others.[12] Ask a question to understand the details, then identify what's in your control to influence or respond to. For example, "Could you help me understand the details of this situation more fully?" Sometimes corrective feedback is accurate but if you perceive that you have little influence on the outcome, you'll be less likely to act, limiting your performance.

Ask "What Went Well?"

If corrective feedback is more like a jug of milk, positive feedback is more like a bottle of wine; it's still delightful even a long time after the event. Receiving positive feedback close to the actual event matters as well, but less so.[13] You're just as likely to learn from delayed positive feedback as you would if they gave you the input right away. Have you ever received a compliment or a note of encouragement months or even years after an event? It's just as motivating as if the event just happened.

Positive feedback doesn't trip our defense mechanisms, so we're more likely to learn from it, regardless of the timing.[14] While corrective feedback is important, we also learn effectively from reinforcing what we do right. John and Julie Gottman, marriage and relationship researchers out of the University of Washington, suggest that feedback in personal relationships should follow a 5 to 1 ratio.[15] According to their research, for every piece of corrective feedback you give, provide five pieces of positive, affirming feedback. Other research in the organizational sciences underscores this principle.[16] We learn from what we did well, not just what we did wrong. Positive feedback matters at work and at home.

Analyzing what is going well actually increases learning more than focusing on the things that are going wrong. Humans receive positive feedback more accurately while corrective feedback can be hard to accept and is more likely to be denied or justified.[17] Positive feedback reinforces what we did well and increases the likelihood that we'll do it again.

Ironically, research also suggests that people are more likely to pay disproportionate attention to corrective feedback.[18] Instead of learning the lessons from positive feedback we often ruminate on corrective feedback. Ask any teacher, professor, or corporate trainer who's received evaluation forms on their instruction from a class. It's always tempting to jump right to the bad news and low scores, even if the positives far outweigh the negatives. It takes deliberate practice to start with the positives. By getting specific about what went well, you also model the importance of celebrating success, creating ongoing motivation for you and your team.

Ask the Right People

There's an ancient proverb that says that an enemy multiplies kisses but that the wounds from a friend can be trusted. One of the keys to effective feedback is the person delivering it. If you receive tough feedback from someone you trust and who you know has your best interests, you are dramatically more likely to receive it. When you get feedback from someone you don't trust or perceive as credible, you're more likely to reject, even if it's accurate.[19] Be thoughtful about the relational investors whom you ask for feedback. Ask people whom you respect and find credible. The best feedback partners are willing to be both tough and tender with you. You know that their feedback isn't a personal attack. They will balance giving you the hard truth with plenty of love, not overemphasizing one or the other. You want feedback from relational investors who are tactful and truthful at the same time, honest and caring.

This is important because as a leader you receive lots of complaints. It can be difficult to remain open to receiving new information, especially if it feels like a personal attack from people who don't understand the full picture. Psychologists suggest that every human has three core psychological needs: autonomy, or the need to make decisions and take personal agency; competence, the need to be and be perceived as capable; and relatedness, the need for genuine relationships with other people.[20] Feedback that feels like a personal attack threatens each of your core psychological needs. Threatening feedback triggers your defensive posture and erodes your self-esteem and confidence.

Who is willing to give you direct feedback still preserving your dignity? My former co-worker, Keith, was one of my feedback partners in the past. He was a peer who I knew had my best interests in mind. He was vested in my success. When he delivered tough feedback that I didn't want to hear, I knew that he was doing it for my good. I'd stop and listen, even if it required the discomfort of changing my behavior or making the effort to apologize to someone. Keith is an example of the relational investor who stretches you with feedback.

The relational investors who stretch you might not be the same people who support you. Sometimes we rely on the same people to provide both feedback and emotional support, but not always. The person you go to get honest, candid input might be a different person than the friend who encourages you and supports you emotionally. That's OK. We often need different people for different developmental needs. Think of the last time you received the right feedback from the wrong person. As one leader reminded me, some people can be so right that they're still wrong. Wisely choose the people you request feedback from. You might have different relational investors who give you stretch, support, or strategy.

Receiving Feedback: Are You Coachable?

If you are approachable, you'll request and create a steady flow of helpful feedback that's critical for eliminating dangerous blind spots. It's one of the key ingredients in becoming a leader who lasts. Over time your actions will be adopted by others. Requesting good feedback is only half of the equation though. If requesting feedback is all about being approachable, receiving feedback is all about being coachable. When someone takes the personal risk to share feedback, demonstrate that you'll put it to work. Here are three approaches for becoming more coachable and turning feedback into performance: reward people, filter feedback, and communicate next steps.

Reward People

How do you respond to feedback? Your attitude sets the tone for your team. One of the most powerful ways to actively promote and encourage giving and receiving feedback in your team is to express gratitude. Thank people when they take the time to provide you with good feedback, especially if that feedback is full of specificity and the person balances honesty and kindness. By rewarding feedback with gratitude, you positively reinforce their behavior, and you lower the risks to future honesty.[21] This deepens trust and increases your performance. Consider these responses:

- "I'm so grateful that you took the time and effort to share that with me. I was completely unaware but now that you brought it to my attention, I'm going to act right away. I'll update you on how it goes."
- "I especially appreciate the specific example that you shared. That makes it more tangible and gives me a better idea about what I might do differently next time."
- "Thanks for sharing that. I can tell it was difficult for you to tell me. The fact that you made the effort means a lot to me. I need to process it a bit more and I'll follow up with a few clarifying questions when I do."

Thanking people for their feedback doesn't mean that you need to agree with it or act on every piece of feedback. On the contrary, wise leaders carefully filter feedback before they plan their next steps. Gratefully receiving feedback signals that you really care about your impact on other people. It looks like careful, active listening with probing, open-ended questions. Your goal is to fully understand all the information available to you. This works personally and professionally. Receiving a steady flow of quality feedback increases awareness you need to become a leader who lasts. Quality feedback reveals your blind spots long before you are at risk for derailing. Receiving feedback involves genuine gratitude and communicating that you'll take the input to heart as you consider next steps.

Filter Feedback

Thanking people for their feedback doesn't mean you need to act on all of it. Jenna was the Chief Operating Officer of a firm with a strong reputation as a market leader. Her role was demanding. Despite her strong performance throughout an organizational transformation, she second guessed herself, never knowing if she was really on the right track. Her boss was verbally supportive of her but led by benevolent absence, largely leaving her alone. She appreciated the trust and autonomy, but she craved actionable feedback to help her stay agile, especially as she increased the scope and scale of her work. She needed more than absent, meaningless praise.

Jenna's shifting role required her to let go of some of the behaviors that made her successful in the past. She had her fingers on the pulse of the organization and had a good sense of the operational headaches. The challenge is that most of what she received was complaints about organizational problems, not feedback for her personal performance. She had to sift very carefully through the issues that came her way to mine any nugget of insight. Without quality input, Jenna spent too much time worrying about whether she was doing the right thing at the right time. If she'd had more clarity about which feedback to act on, she'd likely have increased her confidence and her efficiency. Jenna is an example of the importance of filtering feedback so that you don't waste time and attention by focusing on the things that don't matter the most.

What Jenna came to realize is that soliciting and receiving feedback, doesn't require you to act on everything you hear. There are three active ways to respond when you are confronted with a feedback-performance gap: (a) change your behavior to increase your performance, (b) change the performance standard, or (c) reject the feedback.[22] At the end of the chapter is a brief diagnostic tool to help you filter feedback. Use this framework to filter the feedback that comes your way, saving yourself time and increasing critical areas of self-awareness.

The first option is to change your behavior and close the gap between your desired performance and your actual performance. Step up, work harder, and get better. In many cases, this is the right course. Taking time to understand the issue and identifying specific things to work on can help you change your behavior or help you prioritize what you focus on.

Sometimes you can't increase your performance. Instead, you need to lower the bar for performance, the second option. Often, we or others put self-imposed or arbitrary standards and goals in front of us. If you've tried to rise to the bar but can't, it might be time to consider lowering the bar to a level you can reach. You might have to negotiate with the person giving you feedback. Changing the standard might create the conditions where the feedback you received can make a difference. "I know that we want to increase revenue by 10% this year but based on our numbers from last year, that's not likely to be realistic unless we have a dramatic change in our product offerings. I believe the team can increase revenue by 5% this year. Can we adjust our expectations for our projections?"

Finally, not all feedback is worth acting on. Some feedback you receive is contradictory with other positive feedback. Don't make the mistake of overcorrecting your behavior based on only a few data points. Maybe the person giving you feedback doesn't understand the content or context. Sometimes their feedback is on something relatively unimportant. In those cases, you can gracefully reject the feedback or store it away in case it continues to be verified in the future.

Communicate Next Steps

After you've received and considered feedback carefully, you can act with intention. Anytime you can set a goal based on quality feedback, you increase the impact and likelihood of making a change.[23] The person who brought you the feedback can also be a helpful sounding board for coming up with a viable solution. If you're unsure, just ask. You might be surprised at what they suggest. Once you create intent around your feedback, circle back with the person who gave you feedback to either solicit their advice on your plan of action or just to share an update on your progress. Affirming their efforts to deliver feedback will show your appreciation and keep the channels open for future input.

Building Feedback Rhythms

Relational investors who stretch you with challenging feedback are critical. Leading for the long term requires you to learn things about yourself that are important to change, but difficult to look at in the mirror. When you take the bold steps to lead well you begin to learn how your actions impact others. This has the potential to make you stronger and more effective over the long run but it's not a simple formula for success. It requires relational honesty, personal accountability, and a willingness to sacrifice parts of yourself for the people who rely on you. It requires giving up old habits that might have made you successful in the past to create new capabilities that will take you into the future. The good news is that giving and receiving feedback is a muscle that you can intentionally grow. As your feedback muscles grow, you'll find ways to build feedback rhythms. These habits will become part of your mental frameworks— deep learnings built into your unconscious, automatic processing.

Leaders who last for the long term are attuned to how their actions impact others.

Surround yourself with a circle of relational investors that deliver critical, quality feedback at work and in your personal life. You'll uncover blind spots and increase your effectiveness and ability to perform at your best. If you are in a critical inflection point in your business or career, you can't afford to lead without quality feedback. Don't lead alone. Build a circle that stretches you with feedback.

Reflection Questions

- Consider any recent feedback you've received across your work or your personal life. When was the last time you received helpful feedback? What was it about the feedback, the person, or the environment that made it helpful? How about the last time you received feedback that wasn't helpful? What made that feedback hurt more than it helped?
- What's one area in work or life where you wish you had better information about your performance, both success and growth areas?
- What important feedback might you be ignoring or minimizing?

Take Action: Real-Time Feedback

- Grow your self-awareness by identifying 3–5 people whom you work closely with.
- Personally ask them each individually to reflect on three questions to give you feedback on: (1) How does my attitude or behavior impact you in your work? (2) What do you need more of from me? (3) What do you need less of from me? Consider sending them the questions in advance of meeting so that they can provide you with meaningful feedback.

Take Action: Filter Your Feedback

Directions: Not all feedback is worth acting on. Use this feedback filter tool to assess whether you should accept, negotiate, or reject feedback. Identify a moment that you received feedback and you want to evaluate if you should take action based on it:

Circle YES or NO for each statement below and read the guidance in the gray boxes.

Accept the Feedback If. . .

The issue has a meaningful impact on your performance or someone else's.	YES	NO
There are specific actions that you can take to increase your performance.	YES	NO
You've heard this input from multiple sources and at different points of time.	YES	NO

If you circled YES to two out of the three statements, you might need to accept the feedback and change your behavior so that you can increase your performance.

Negotiate the Feedback If. . .

Performance standards are unrealistically high and won't likely be met anytime soon.	YES	NO
The measure of success is self-imposed and not a true indication of success.	YES	NO
Lowering the standard will make success attainable, but still keep it challenging.	YES	NO

If you circled YES to two out of the three statements, you might need to lower the bar for performance expectations. You might need to negotiate those standards with someone else.

Reject the Feedback If. . .

The feedback source isn't credible or it's something outside of your control.	YES	NO
You've received overwhelmingly positive, contradictory feedback.	YES	NO
The issue is minor and not worth spending time or effort on at this time.	YES	NO

5 | Ideas: The Perspective Advantage

Key Takeaways

- Innovation is a competitive edge in a rapidly changing world. Relational investors who stretch your perspective develop your mental flexibility and ignite new ideas and divergent ways of thinking and acting.
- The perspective advantage comes from a circle of relational investors that guides you through the unknown and spurs your creativity in the process. These critical relationships bring you new ideas to fuel your business as you scale.
- CEOs who get advice from diverse networks outside their industry had stronger company performance and valuation. The ideal type of network for new, creative invention is made up of "loose connections," a diverse group of people whom you probably don't know well but who spur new ideas.

- The ideal circle for innovation and rapid iteration is a smaller group of relational investors who challenge your thinking but support your processing.
- Increase your ability to lead with creativity by prioritizing "catalyst conversations" with relational investors from a wide range of industries, in divergent fields or from widely different walks of life.

The world of work is changing rapidly. Many leaders even consider today to be a new industrial revolution.[1] Global markets and rapid technology advances are only part of the story. Every organization faces an ongoing need to constantly iterate and evolve, shifting priorities to keep pace. With so much dynamic change, leaders are required to create and innovate more than any other time in history. Leading a business has plenty of challenges already. In the face of unpredictable shifts, adding the need to constantly transform can be daunting.

If you want to be a leader who stands the test of time, then innovation is critical. If you need to generate novel, creative solutions or drive innovation then you need a circle of relational investors who challenge your biases. You need an idea network. These relational investors stretch you and stimulate you to think in novel, innovative ways or to see things differently than before. They help you push the boundaries of your assumptions about the world.

In this chapter, we'll discover a new relational investor, people who stretch your perspective and spur new ideas. We'll explore the perspective advantage and learn how perspective complements feedback. We'll define the difference between invention and innovation, and we'll look at how different relational investors can help us achieve different goals. We'll look at how to start catalyst conversations that spark your creativity. Most important, you'll surround yourself with a critical set of relational investors to help you become a leader who lasts.

The Perspective Advantage

Leaders who last learn how to navigate unpredictable change. Relational investors who stretch your perspective provide a competitive advantage for you personally in your career and organizationally for the places where you lead. Innovating companies generate more value. Relational investors who stretch your perspective develop your mental flexibility and ignite new ideas and divergent ways of thinking and acting. They help you get ahead of disruption in a fast-paced, dynamic world. The perspective advantage comes from a circle of relational investors that guides you through the unknown and spurs your creativity in the process. These critical relationships bring you new ideas. They keep you aware and awake as a leader. They also stretch the way you think. The best part is that you probably already know who these people are, but you haven't tapped into their genius yet. Here are two examples of the perspective advantage at work.

Derrick, a Chief Revenue Officer, had been tasked with creating the next-level business model for a business that had a software product and that offered professional services. He knew that his own visibility into the options was limited. To get a sense of the range of possibilities, he created a list of 12 leaders in firms that were different than his but that all shared at least one similar element to his business.

Derrick already knew these leaders, but he hadn't reached out to ask their opinion yet. He identified them because they could give him new perspectives and fresh ways of thinking about how his company sold and delivered their product. The conversations he engaged in uncovered opportunities and challenges he'd never considered. But the real value for Derrick came through the crosspollination of novel ideas as he received rich, diverse ideas.

This exercise helped him generate a unique hybrid business model that he hadn't seen in the market before. The new model built off the lessons he learned from others and the emerging trends he was seeing in the market but it also custom fit the unique nuances of his business. The owners of his business were thrilled at the new market strategy that Derrick generated. This positioned him for future equity leadership roles.

Enlisting the help of these different leaders brought Derrick information but it also changed the way he approached the challenge in front of him. The fun part was that each person was excited to help him and share the lessons they'd learned, many by painful trial and error. They also connected him to other people whom he didn't know, expanding his perspective and bridging to connections outside of his available network. Their generosity and support propelled his creativity as he developed new pathways to reimagine a product and service that makes a meaningful and sustainable impact in the lives of people.

Creating is an important part of what it means to be human. It's powerful to experience as a leader. The people who invest in you to expand your boundaries will feel a meaningful and motivational intrinsic reward as well. It feels good to get into the flow with someone when the creative sparks start to fly.

What Derrick experienced is something that globally recognized design firm IDEO discovered a long time ago. Pioneers in human-centered design, IDEO has been providing innovative solutions to an impressive range of industries for more than 40 years. Landmark creations such as early work for Steve Jobs at Apple put them on the map but their methodology for creation has kept them at the forefront of innovation.

One of the cornerstones of their process is bringing together individuals from a wide range of divergent disciplines to solve multi-dimensional and multidisciplinary problems. By pulling a broad range of disciplines together, they can harness expertise from a myriad of perspectives. Moving beyond single points of view, the challenges that they tackle bring fresh, integrative thinking that they apply to product design, to business models, to social issues, to educational systems and much more. Taking concepts out of silos can infuse new thinking and challenge old assumptions about the way things have always been.

An example of this was seen in a collaborative project between researchers from the University of Central Florida, Arizona State University, and the University of Michigan to explore the link between network diversity and organizational performance.[2] They looked at the extent to which CEOs get outside of their available networks for advice from other top-level leaders and the relationship with the performance of their firm. They found that CEOs who get advice from top leaders whom they don't know and aren't similar—for example, someone from a different industry or from a different discipline or background—had stronger firm performance and value. The CEOs who had access to novel points of view increased the objective quality of their decisions, impacting the performance of their organizations.

Relational investors who challenge and change your perspective can help you stay ahead of change or at least keep pace with the ambiguity around you. The exciting lesson from how IDEO convenes and cultivates creativity is that you don't need to have a world-class design firm on call to start expanding your perspective through conversations that activate your thinking and stretch your capabilities.

Mirrors and Windows

Healthy leaders surround themselves with relationships for stretch, support, and strategy. When it comes to stretch, these relational investors provide you with perspective—new and different ways of seeing the world. Like feedback in Chapter 4, this part of your trust circle opens possibilities for you to consider. But the two networks are different. Feedback and perspective overlap in that they open the opportunity for your self-awareness and awareness of others and the world. As my friend and serial entrepreneur Bob Lambert says, you need someone on your board of advisors who gives you contrarian points of view and fills in the gaps in what you cannot see. The difference is in the direction of insight and perspective. When it comes to relationships that stretch, some people are like mirrors, and some are like windows.

The people in your feedback network often serve as mirrors. Any time I am acting in a way that isn't aligned with my values, there are a few key people in my family and at work who will graciously or forcefully help me see what I really look like. They provide input on where I might need to change.

Several years ago, our house flooded, and my wife and I lived through an extended season with small children in a hotel. The open layout of the hotel room meant that I couldn't turn on the light in our bathroom early in the morning. The light would stream into the bedroom, waking our young kids far too early. This meant that I ended up having to get dressed in the dark, every morning. I couldn't see what I looked like in the mirror. Every couple of days I'd have to laugh as I'd end up wearing shirts and pants that were a different color than what I had intended to wear. On occasion, I'd have to sneak back into the room to change my clothes before heading off to lead an offsite session. Feedback, like a mirror, is critical and it shows us what we really look like, strengths and growth areas.

Similarly, these relational investors also provide perspective, but not in the same way as the mirror. This part of your circle operates more like a large, expansive picture window frame. If you've ever had a favorite lounge spot to sit at in your home or at a coffee shop, then you've experienced this. The window draws your gaze outside of the built environment into the expanse in the distance. Instead of looking at yourself, your focus is projected away from you at the new possibilities.

Relational investors who stretch you often include mirrors who help you see yourself more clearly and windows that provide perspective expanding views into places you might go. Like the rest of your circle, some people will fill multiple roles, providing both feedback and perspective, self-reflection, and future inspiration.

Chris Nicholas needed a fresh perspective when he hit an inflection point in his career. The healthcare system he worked in had a leadership gap at the top and he'd just been named head of one of the largest hospital units. There was also the $140 million deficit to deal with. It felt overwhelming. During a virtual call, a consultant noticed Chris struggling and challenged him with a new perspective. The consultant stopped him mid-meeting with blunt honesty: "You don't seem very engaged. If you're not engaged, how do you expect anyone else to row in the same direction?" It was hard to hear, but Chris needed to be brought back to what mattered. The consultant didn't stop at honest feedback; he urged Chris to seek the clinical high ground, anchoring his team in the higher purpose they served and the impact they had in the community. That moment shifted Chris's focus toward solving the crisis. Today, only a few years later, the hospital is financially sustainable and has a 10-year strategic plan for impact and healthy growth. Chris was able to be a key part of the turnaround. He also shared a metaphor around losing 20 pounds that shaped his thinking during this leadership challenge. He described that there are four ways to lose 20 pounds. Leaders can cut off a leg (slash resources), do liposuction (eliminate services), starve themselves (austerity), or get fit for the mission (build sustainable systems). The first three options weaken the system and prevent the team from serving the community. The latter takes the most work but it makes the most difference. It became his focus and his new viewpoint for leading from a place of purpose. Today, these lessons have imprinted on Chris's leadership philosophy and it all started with a new point of view.

Who are the windows in your life at home or at work? Who helps you think in new and different ways that open possibilities? These people are likely already around you, just waiting to be asked to contribute their thoughts. Some of these people stretch your thinking even further by setting up a telescope in the window, giving you a far-reaching perspective that can change the trajectory of your work.

I witnessed one of these trajectory changing experiences in my leadership role as the Chief Commercial Officer at WiLD Leaders Inc., a leadership firm that pioneered a system for measuring and building trust, with the tagline and brand promise "Leadership = Trust, Now You Can Measure It, Now You Can Build It." As our leadership team built the business, we experienced many reflective moments that provided us feedback and input, but we also had some special moments that carried our gaze forward to places we'd not seen.

One important moment was the genesis of the WiLD Foundation. Beth, a friend of the firm and the Executive Director of a hospital foundation, encouraged Dr. McKenna, the founder, to consider setting up a not-for-profit entity alongside our business to serve in unique ways that the business wouldn't be able to meet. She explained how hospitals have been doing that for years, creating multiple funding pathways for different populations. She described how a 501c3 could parallel the business to serve organizations that have a desperate need for deep-seated leader development but often lack the resources necessary to make the investment needed. Her suggestion triggered new thinking in our founder and five years later, the WiLD Foundation existed alongside WiLD Leaders Inc. serving different populations of leaders. The idea for this model, novel to us, had existed in other industries for a long time. All we needed was the catalyzing conversation with a relational investor.

Invention Versus Innovation

When you think about the relationships that help expand your thinking, it's important to distinguish between relationships that spur invention versus relationships that spur innovation. The process of invention often requires a novel discovery, ideation, or creation. True inventions, products, or philosophies are original with little to no prior history. Innovation differs from invention in that innovations result through the process of refining, adapting, or building upon something that was already in existence.

Much of what we see today is iterative innovation. As the writer of the ancient book of Ecclesiastes wrote more than two and a half-millennia ago, there is often nothing new under the sun. Still, these relationships can provide the perspective you need to make a breakthrough or iterate faster and in the right direction.

The relational investors who challenge your perspective can help you with both creative invention and iterative innovation, but the research on development networks and creativity suggests that there is a slightly different type of network for each outcome. Just like the rest of your circle of relational investors, you'll need different people around you for different reasons. Generally, research shows that the ideal type of network that generates invention and novel creativity is made up of "loose connections," people whom you know, but not necessarily well.[3] A wide, large network supports this because you become connected to individuals who bridge "structural holes" in your network.[4] Think about a physical bridge that connects two different bodies of land together. In the same way, there are relational brokers who can socially bridge us into networks with ideas and perspectives that we didn't have access to on our own. This widely divergent network triggers new thinking, resulting in the opportunity to ideate and invent new ways of doing things.

Innovation is also driven by loose connections but as the creative journey evolves it also requires people to help implement innovation—a group of tight knit supporters who continue to challenge your thinking but also support you along the way.[5] Having a wide network brings fresh, new ideas, but you don't have to have a sprawling network to harvest the benefits of a different perspective. Research by Markus Baer from Washington University in St. Louis suggests that you likely only need around a dozen, diverse acquaintance level relationships whom you engage with periodically to get your creativity going.[6] The key is taking the effort of intentionally setting up conversations that will challenge your thinking and marshal your energy forward.

Catalyst Conversations

In the same way that travel expands your thinking, conversations with people in your perspective network foster the conditions for creative juices to flow. Prioritize conversations with relational investors from diverse industries, in divergent fields, or from widely different walks of life. To increase your ability to lead with creativity, get outside of your own viewpoint to generate new ideas. Do you have a friend who was trained in a completely different field than you? Who do you know who has a view of the world that's different from yours?

These unlikely characters could be the most likely to open your thinking or offer an unconventional approach.

PATH, a global not-for-profit organization focused on health and technology, is tackling some of the toughest community and global health issues of our day, from malaria to Ebola, through innovation and technology. A large part of their plan has been innovating and deploying technology in partnership with private industry, NGOs, and government agencies. One of the keys to their success is the way that they structure their teams. A PATH team working on the research and development of a new medicine or medical device includes at least three people: a scientist or technologist, a global/community health specialist, and a commercialization officer. This unique combination means that every technology will be developed and shepherded to the global market with multiple perspectives throughout the process.

Catalyst conversations are built into the process. The scientist or technologist is responsible for making sure that the actual innovation works in a practical way, the health specialist contributes contextual awareness of how a community might receive or react to a technology, and the commercialization officer sits at the intersection of these two points and brings expertise in how to bring the technology to market and distribute it effectively, in terms of cost and scale.

Conventional approaches keep these verticals in separate silos and follow a more linear hand-off approach. Here is the typical picture: a scientist develops an effective solution for fighting a disease. After optimizing the science, they then pass it off to a business office to commercialize and deploy to the market. The commercialization team works on the business side of the endeavor and gets everything in line to distribute the solution.

Finally, a community health professional is given the solution with instructions on how to administer it safely and effectively. Everyone is excited to see how the solution will make a difference in the health of the target community. Imagine the surprise that the science team and the business team discover when they find that the solution, though technically effective and distributed efficiently, didn't fit with the lifestyle or preferences of the target population and adoption rates turn out to be abysmal.

Scenarios like this happen every day. By bringing the divergent parts of the value chain together, PATH's ideation happens in an interconnected and integrated way. This ensures that solutions are not only technologically effective but readily adopted, fitting the true needs of a population. Even more, the solutions are designed in scalable ways that maximize the value for the cost.

What PATH has succeeded in is the systematization of catalyst conversations that give birth to novel ideas. Every team has its own built-in idea network that generates new perspectives, whether they realize it or not. These conversations also provide the ongoing support to bring those ideas to fruition and then to scale. As PATH states, they "specialize in developing, introducing, and scaling up solutions to the world's most pressing health challenges."[7] If the most pressing, complex global health concerns are being tackled by innovative, interdisciplinary teams, what would change for your team or organization if you systematically got outside of the walls of your own perspective to spur innovation and carry ideas to the finish line? As you fill your circle with people for perspective, it can transform your team as well.

A Fresh Frame of Reference

One of the best parts of these types of catalyst conversations is that they not only challenge your thinking, but you get drawn into an exchange of ideas. Catalyst conversations are marked by a *reciprocal* and *recursive* mix of learning and sharing. These conversations are reciprocal because as you learn you end up sharing as well, guaranteeing that both parties walk away with new perspectives. But that's not where the magic of catalyst conversations stops. The recursive part of these conversations means that these discussions spark ideas that in turn spark other ideas. Engaging in the development and activation of new perspectives means that any time you invest in these relationships is truly developmental for you as a leader. Expanding your perspective builds your capacity now and again into the future. In the same way that strength training builds stronger muscle that allows you to then build stronger muscle, relational investors that stretch your perspective set your creativity into motion. As you crosspollinate these ideas across different perspectives, the inventions and innovations will generate on their own. It's one of the reasons that people who we perceive as "creative" always appear to have a steady stream of inspiration. These leaders have activated a recursive chain reaction that's beyond reciprocity.

The most energizing catalyst conversations allow you and the others to "talk shop" and share the projects you are working on, or the concepts you are playing with. There is often no direct competition so you can let your guard down and free form, creating something interesting as you go. These conversations also help you push past your own bias. It's been documented that people are much more likely to seek confirming evidence than disconfirming evidence.[8] Getting diverse perspectives across industry, discipline, age, race, socioeconomic status, political viewpoint, or any other category, opens your world and helps you see the more complete picture. It's why some business leaders I know have shifted from static "market research" to dynamic and ongoing "market listening." At The Sage Group®, we call this The Mind of the Market™ because we provide our clients with persistent, ongoing insights into their ecosystem so that they can take advantage before their competition by seeing what's seemingly unseen. This posture goes beyond just gathering data to truly understanding deeper needs and motivators.

Brad Jackson, CEO of the award-winning consulting firm, Slalom, is a role model for this way of approaching relationships. Brad is known for big ideas. He leads a consulting firm that approaches the market in a different way than its competitors. Brad is a voracious learner and always on the hunt for new ideas, perspectives, and opinions. He surrounds himself with experts from fields outside his own or that of his firm. He even has a dedicated staff member to help him create technology prototypes to some of the ideas that come to him.

Like any inventor, some ideas stick, some don't. Regardless, the discipline of curiosity, expressed in asking questions of people with different viewpoints, refines his thinking and challenges his assumptions. For Slalom, it's meant that a different model has attracted top talent from larger organizations. It's also imprinted a spirit of creation and entrepreneurship into the culture. Leaders who join the firm can continue to operate outside the conventional bounds of consulting and professional services, igniting their own creativity.

Instant Community and Connection: Executive Peer Groups

When it comes to gaining perspective and generating new ideas one of the most powerful formats for accelerating community is the executive peer advisory movement—an organized format to give executives a circle of relational investors. A seasoned and storied leader, the Advisory Board Chair, will assemble a group of leaders or business owners together across divergent industries and backgrounds to form an informal advisory board where 10–15 executives can bring real challenges across their work and life for support, stretch, and challenge. The Chair facilitates monthly advisory offsites, helps leaders create cases for their members to get structured feedback from other leaders, and fosters a place for leaders to process the intersection of life with their business. Most executive peer advisory groups intentionally pull leaders from divergent industries for catalyst conversations that keep perspectives fresh. Most group leaders will create structured time for you to bring your challenges and opportunities to your peers for input and to test your assumptions.[9]

Why do peer advisory groups work? Greg Leith, the former CEO of Convene—a large, faith-driven peer advisory, captured it perfectly "Real learning happens over time in community." Executive peer groups bring instant connection, stretch, support, and strategy. Most formats include coaching with the chair. Many groups create such deep levels of trust that members stay together for decades. One national network of tight knit business owners from diverse industries describe their forums as Community on Demand, because that's what it's about at the core. Peer networks provide instant relationships. Most importantly, leaders realize they aren't alone, and they have people to lean on for perspective when they need it.

Long-Term Perspective

Where do you need a different perspective in your life? Who can provide you with a surprising and fresh frame of reference? It might not be the people you'd first expect. By investing in this part of your circle, you'll be stretched in a perspective expanding way that helps you look out and see possibilities that you didn't know existed. As complexity increases and clarity wanes, the ability to generate ongoing innovation can help you keep or set the pace of change and impact. This is what author and futurist Brian Evergreen calls "Future Solving" instead of problem solving. Investing in this part of your circle of relational investors spurs new ideas but it also changes the way you think. Matt Skarin and Ron Worman, partners of mine in The Sage Group®, are two of those people. They see opportunities that I don't perceive, and their thinking stretches my own, causing me to consider possibilities that I hadn't before. The long-term edge in leading effectively is your ability to learn and grow. Relational investors who change your perspective give you that advantage.

A healthy trust circle includes a mix of similarity and diversity. Relational investors who change our thinking allow us to feel boundaryless, if only for moments. When we get outside our own heads, we start to experience a core part of the human experience, the ability to take what is around us and invent and innovate. We produce new value that can make an impact on the lives of people around us or beyond us. Dynamic change and uncertainty might be what triggers leaders to get new perspectives, but the very act of creating and making may be what sustains it. Lead for the long term by surrounding yourself with fresh perspectives.

> **Reflection Questions**
>
> - Who has stretched your thinking and challenged your assumptions in the past? Who are the people that unlock your ability to think in innovative ways? How did they do that? What are the characteristics of those people?
> - What was the last thing that you created or improved? What was meaningful about that experience for you?
> - Where in your life do you need a fresh perspective? Why?

Take Action: Catalyst Conversations

- Start a series of catalyst conversations to spur creativity and innovation. Identify one project that you are working on where you need a new perspective. Who are three people who think or do things radically differently than you? Start a conversation with them and share what you are working on. Get ready for insights and ideas that you've not considered before. Some of the ideas you receive will take shape, others won't. The goal is to unlock your thinking and provide you a new perspective.

Support

Leadership requires resilience and fortitude. It's common for leaders to shoulder responsibility and weather crises without having a safe place to recover or people to guide them along the way. Leaders need relationships that support them at some point in their journey. Relational investors who support help you to move beyond isolation by giving you a sense of safety and by providing valuable advice for decisions.

Many leaders fall into the trap of trying to lead on their own, without the encouragement and counsel of others. Asking for help can be difficult. It requires a leader to honestly come to terms with the fact that they are limited in their wisdom and capacity and that they need others to surround them and hold them up. Asking for help also requires that a leader has people who are safe to approach. This includes people who will suspend judgement and allow the leader to process their experiences. It also includes people who can provide timely insights from their own experience. Because of the need for safety, it's especially important to get relational support from people who aren't inside the organization in which you lead. Having a mix of internal support and external support allows a leader to get both contextual, just-in-time encouragement or perspective as well as objective input that isn't biased by organizational culture.

The research is clear that when leaders are supported, it creates a powerful buffer for stress that creates leadership sustainability. Leaders need relationships that stretch them to grow their capacity and increase their performance. But without relationships that support, leaders will bend till they break. Leaders who last are leaders who are surrounded by supportive relational investors. In this section we will focus on two relationships that support, the role of people who support us emotionally (Chapter 6) and the importance of mentors (Chapter 7).

People who provide you emotional support might be friends, family, or even peers at work. These people are safe harbors. You can move beyond the guise of self-sufficiency and become truly transparent and authentic. These relationships aren't focused on delivering you advice, even though you might find that a sounding board helps you gain clarity. In a world marked by surface-level connections, relationships that provide emotional support present the gift of presence and attention, moments when you can pause and be who you are, warts and all, to move forward with intention.

Mentors can provide social and emotional support to protégés as well, but the value of a mentor is delivered through guidance, advice, and perspective from someone who has often gone before you in a particular area of life. A mentor might provide advice on an important career decision or impart practical knowledge on how to grow a specific skill or ability. You might even rely on a mentor to navigate parenting or leading in your family. Mentors share the wealth of their experience and model what success looks like.

Building leadership endurance requires that we get surrounded by people whom we can be honest with, people who will encourage us, guide us, and model the way forward. Let's get surrounded by people who support us as we support others.

6

Emotional Support: The Safe Harbor in Any Storm

Key Takeaways

- You need relational investors who emotionally support you and provide encouragement to continue pressing forward, especially when challenges arise.
- Many leaders fall prey to the hero complex and work tirelessly to provide for the needs of others only to find that they are running on empty and ready to crash.
- Leaders who last are the ones who seek out relational investors to provide the emotional and psychological support needed to give them the strength to stand up another day.
- There are two psychological pitfalls that keep leaders from taking the initiative to ask relational investors for emotional support: (1) the fallacy of self-sufficiency and (2) the perception of connectedness.

■ Getting emotional support takes tremendous humility. To combat the fallacies that you believe about yourself requires you to step out and ask for help.

There are certain laws of nature that are relentlessly true no matter how hard we might push against them. The ocean tide ebbs and flows and ebbs again, in constant rhythm with the gravitational pull of the moon. We can do nothing to stop it, or gravity for that matter. The second law of thermodynamics states that events tend toward disorder and chaos unless acted upon. Similarly, the need for leaders to have emotional relational support will always be a constant for leaders across the globe and throughout time. Even leaders who believe that they are surrounded by relational support will find that these connections will weaken and dissipate over time if not actively tended. Who provides you with emotional support? These people are the relational investors you would call if your life or career were crumbling.

If you are in leadership then you will always have deep needs for emotional support. Knowing that you have a supportive community of care is a powerful way to keep you resilient in the middle of storms. As we saw in earlier chapters, surrounding yourself with people for stretch will propel you to the next level in your journey as a leader. Stretch is a critical ingredient for development but the relationships that emotionally support you are the foundation that enables growth.

Relational investors who emotionally support you provide encouragement to continue pressing forward, especially when challenges arise. We've already seen that too much stretch without support only causes leaders to break.[1] Many leaders unintentionally self-sabotage and miss out on the care that people are ready and willing to provide. In this chapter, we'll discover the importance of relational investors who provide emotional support. These people serve as safe harbors for you during storms. We'll uncover two psychological dangers that get in the way of getting the support you need, the fallacy of self-sufficiency and the perception of connectedness. Lastly, we'll look at how to access relational investors for emotional support by cultivating intentionality and humility.

Every Leader Needs a Safe Harbor

Big Wayne is a big guy with a big personality. A former Naval Officer and Naval Academy graduate who stands at 6'8"—but he'll tell you he is 5'20"—Wayne is a strong leader who cares for his people, and he's created a uniquely valuable business in the airline parts space. When you meet Wayne, you can't picture that he has bad days. He's the type of leader that sees potential and takes initiative with energy. He also has the wisdom to think strategically. I can imagine Wayne as a leader from the moment he was on the playground as a child.

But Wayne also knows the dangers of leading and impact of isolation. He describes leadership as a responsibility that's too big to carry alone. To create his own sustainability, he's put together an ecosystem of relationships to fit the needs that he has across his life. He calls them layers of relational support. The first layer is his what he calls his "personal board of directors," which includes Jesus, his wife, and two highly trusted friends (a pastor and a Christian university president). This team gives him personal and spiritual counsel. Second, he has a Peer Advisory Team through Convene where he receives corporate-level problem solving, sound advice, and collaborative input and collective wisdom on important decisions. Third, he has outside support with a professional executive coach for objective feedback and leadership sharpening. Finally, he has a corporate board in his business for strategic oversight and accountability. Wayne has different people who support him in the ways he needs. He honestly shared that during one of the most difficult phases of his life, he added the care of a therapist to give him some tools to keep his mental state strong and focused. He wisely noted that often, successful leaders can struggle because their persistence can easily turn into rumination, creating a feeling that they are never doing enough. Wayne's confidence comes from who he is, but it also comes from who he's surrounded himself with. He's a capable leader, but he has the humility to ask for help from others and to enlist the talents of his team members to get things done. His intentionality buffers him from the risks of lonely leadership.

Leading, by its very nature, is an isolating activity. If you are leading anywhere where the stakes are even remotely high, then you are at a greater risk for isolation and loneliness.[2] The greater your levels of responsibility, the greater your likelihood of feeling alone. You are regularly required to make decisions that people disagree with. You also hold increasing levels of sensitive information. At the same time, greater responsibility as a leader means that you have increased needs to be surrounded by people who can be a safe harbor for you.

The realities of leading create a greater need to rely on others. At the same time there can be false pressure that makes you feel like you should be able to do it all on your own. You deeply need real and authentic connection with people whom you can be honest with. Authenticity with the people you lead can be meaningful, up to a point. There are many things that you can't share with the people you lead, even if you wanted to. Sometimes you keep information in confidence for legal reasons, other times for personal reasons. More often it's that you are working to create the conditions for others to thrive and flourish and working to be thoughtful with sensitive information.

It's easy to fall prey to the hero complex and work tirelessly to provide for the needs of others only to find that you are running on empty and ready to crash. For many leaders, these reflective realizations often come in the rear-view mirror after a spectacular derailment or a slow-burning fade. Hero or not, the organization usually keeps on going in some way without you.

This was the trajectory that Mary was on. She was the CEO of a technology consultancy that she was charged with getting ready for sale. The organization had tremendous potential to maximize valuation. After three years her efforts were starting to pay off. She received praise from the board for her tough decision-making and she was just seeing the fruit of her hard work as she drove the team forward. As the first quarter of 2020 approached its close, a global pandemic hit, COVID-19. Overnight, her business went from heading in the right direction to heading in the wrong direction. Mary's supportive board seemed to suddenly forget her recent wins. Mary was pressed by fear and anxiety from both sides. She suddenly had to navigate how to be accountable to a board for environmental changes outside her control while at the same time pressing forward with confidence and clarity with her team who clamored for a bit of certainty, something she couldn't provide without lying.

In the middle of the chaos, Mary took a risk and finally admitted to her executive team that she was struggling. She confessed that she just needed even a little bit of appreciation for how hard she was working to hold on for the people who depended on her from all sides. Until that moment, Mary had been suffering in silence with no one to check in on how she was doing. It was a risky move on her part to descend into authenticity with her team. That moment provided a bit of a release, but it was quickly back to the status quo with the demands and pace of a turnaround in a world that had been turned upside down. While her team was supportive, they ultimately didn't feel the weight of her burden to the same level that she did.

Mary's story highlights the importance of having relational investors who are supporting you. Often, your relational investors for support might be outside of your organization. The pressure that Mary faced was enormous and she simply needed someone who could encourage her. It took Mary time, but she got surrounded by support, made it through the storm, and took the business to market, successfully getting acquired by a larger firm.

Releasing the Pressure

The stress and tensions that leading can create require a pressure release valve—even for the most seasoned leaders, whether they love where they lead or not. Leaders need people whom they can fully be themselves with. People who are safe emotional harbors. People whom they can open themselves to about what's really going on. This isn't about merely having a friend to complain to or to vent about the stresses of work. It's much more than that. It can be hard to articulate how you are really doing. This is about people who are psychologically safe to be around. You can take an emotional or relational risk with them without fearing any repercussions.

It's about knowing that you aren't alone and that others see you, know you, and have your best interests in mind. It's a rare place where judgement is suspended and where your decisions aren't scrutinized and challenged.

These are people whom you can process the real and gritty parts of your world with. They are more likely to ask you questions, without an agenda, than provide you with pithy answers or simple solutions. Yes, you might cry on their shoulders from time to time, but the most powerful thing that they offer is the tangible reminder that you are not alone. You have permission to let down your guard. These are people who will just be with you when you need it. Just their presence brings you comfort and provides hope. Knowing that you are supported as a leader can create a tremendous amount of resolve and resiliency for the pressure that you are facing.

Every leader, at some point, encounters a dark night of the soul. Did I make the right decision? Am I in the right role? Do I have what it takes? What happens if I fail? What should I do next? It doesn't matter how strong and self-reliant you might appear to be. If you are honest, you have moments that test your resolve and leave you feeling uncertain about whether you are qualified to lead or whether you can provide what the people who follow you need.

It's been my experience that leaders at all levels, no matter the context, are starving for real and meaningful connection with people who are willing to step into their mess. Leaders need relational investors to provide the emotional and psychological support needed to give them the strength to stand up another day. If you are supporting others, it can be important to stop and make sure you have people who are supporting you.

Jeremy needed supporting relationships like this. He is an academic leader who runs a private university that has been having financial struggles for several years. Today, he is faced with the devastating possibility of shutting down the institution where hundreds of his friends and colleagues work. This is the place where he and his wife met as students together. It's the place where thousands of alumni have had lives enriched and transformed. For him, the possibility of shutting the institution down isn't just about buildings and budgets. It runs much deeper. Business is personal.

But whom can he talk to on his staff or his executive team about the overwhelming, isolating pressure that he is feeling? He is living all the tensions and expectations of leading, in real-time. As one of his executive advisors, I realized that an important part of my role was simply to be there for him and to encourage him to lead with strength and care in the difficult situation he found himself in.

Leading is tough. And if nothing else, I hope that reading this gives you permission to breathe deep and know that you are not alone. It's OK to ask for help. Just knowing that our experience isn't unique gives us a strange sense of hope during storms. There are relational investors who are ready, willing, and able to support us and to help us process the pressure, if only we'd ask. In my work with leaders, I've observed two psychological pitfalls that keep leaders from taking the initiative to ask relational investors for emotional support: the fallacy of self-sufficiency and the perception of connectedness.

The Fallacy of Self-Sufficiency

One of the great fallacies of leading is that you must do it alone and that to reach out for help or emotional support denotes weakness or incompetence. It's almost the first unwritten rule that you learn about leading. The fallacy of the self-sufficient leader is dangerous and pervasive. It's understandable too. People rely on you and the ways that you think, feel, and behave have real consequences. You quickly learn that people pay closer attention to your language, interpreting or misinterpreting what you say. Your words have greater weight as a leader, like it or not.

We mistakenly believe that because leadership requires strength that there is no room for weakness. The reality is that we all need help. No leader has all the capabilities required for any job. Take a closer look at the next job posting you come across for a senior leadership role. I'm always amazed when I read line-item after line-item of requirements, pedigree, skill, and experience. It's as if any candidate must be a superhuman who walks on water and is perfectly unflappable in every situation, yet compassionate and connected to the needs of their people at the same time.

It's both arrogant and foolish to assume that we are self-sufficient and that we have all we need as leaders. This is a step toward derailment. Leading is sure to make us come face to face with our inadequacies. Most of us are not fully equipped for the dynamic changes and unprecedented challenges that we might face or the shockwaves of our decisions or the decisions of others that we might still need to shoulder. Leading is tough. Even if your role as a leader likely has deep purpose and meaning, it can also emotionally drain you and leave you feeling empty. Many leaders experience this daily, but they just grit their teeth and bear through it. No leader should suffer in silence.

Self-sufficiency is a dangerous leadership fallacy. People need you to lead and to lead sustainably. People rely on you, and they need you to be at your best. In every corner of our world there is a shortage of leaders. Ignoring your needs for supportive relationships ignores an essential part of what it means to be human. When we do this, we deceive ourselves and we unintentionally reduce our capacity to lead at the same time.

If you are navigating the challenges of scale, sale, or succession, you will be confronted with your inability to lead alone as your fortitude is tested. There are too many moving parts to pay attention to and too many factors that can go the wrong way. I've been surprised many times to discover that one of the most valuable things I've given to clients in these crucible moments is simply my presence and availability. The real relational connection never shows up in a proposal or statement of work, but I sometimes discover that it's the deeper reason I'm there.

My friend Adam was a leader who successfully fought the fallacy of self-sufficiency. He was the top leader of a family foundation focused on investing in the local community. His organization was growing. Over five focused years he had become an integral part of the community that he served. He also had some staffing issues. A particular relationship with one of his employees suddenly went south. The situation turned very ugly, and it kept him awake every night. As he described the gut-wrenching experience, I could viscerally feel his pain. He was working hard to care for this individual whom he would need to ultimately fire from his organization. Adam was being sabotaged by his disgruntled team member behind his back. Still, he was working hard to maintain respect and candor with kindness. At the same time, he was striving to hold confidentiality with his team. Because of the nature of the issues with his difficult team member, no one else on the team knew the details and therefore couldn't understand why their colleague was getting fired.

Knowing my friend well, I'd seen his calm demeanor under pressure and his efforts to always treat people with respect. I also know that he cares about people. This situation had been difficult for him. I asked him what had kept him anchored in the middle of the experience he'd just emerged from. He told me that the thing that kept him pressing on was the incredible network of support that he was surrounded with. He had invested in building a rich circle of people to share his struggles in confidentiality. He was part of a peer group of executives, and he had close confidants in his faith community. Each person was committed to encourage him and remind him of his purpose and the mission he was on. This incredible level of support buoyed his spirits and fueled his resolve to lean into the mess and honestly evaluate his own strengths and limitations as well as the merits and consequences of his decisions.

Adam had access to a rich circle of relational investors for social and emotional support. He recognized his emotional needs and actively took advantage of the care that was offered to him. The challenge he faced tested his resolve and his integrity even when he was being publicly slandered. During this experience, his relational investors reminded him of who he was, why he took the job in the first place, and what his higher purpose was through the mission of this organization. While this didn't change the sleepless nights, it did mean that he had a hope that cut through the fog of the situation to give him a beam of light into the future. He emerged as a stronger leader, still full of compassion, and more equipped to lead for the long term.

We need people who can help us be who we most truly are—friends, family, or colleagues. These are people who remind you about your deepest identity—because they know you. These are people who pause to carefully consider how to support you in uncharted territory—because they don't pretend that they have all the answers. These are people who can remind you of the purpose that you are on and put wind in your sails, time after time. Often, they are right in front of us, waiting for us to make the first move. Don't miss the opportunity to ask for help and support. Having people available to you is different than intentionally accessing their support.

The Perception of Connectedness

Some leaders don't struggle with the fallacy of self-sufficiency. Many leaders are fully aware of their limitations but unaware of whom they can rely on. The second pitfall for getting emotional support is the perception of connectedness. One of the first conversations you have in Psychology 101 is the difference between perception and reality. It continues to be an interesting topic for lively dinner debates. When it comes to getting the support we need as leaders, the difference between perception and reality has the potential to derail us. The perception of connectedness leads us to believe that we have a network of emotionally supportive, developmental relationships when indeed we don't. This false perception can prevent us from making the intentional effort needed to foster relationships where we are both giving care and receiving it.

In a hyper-connected age, our ability to be attuned to everyone we know on social media is one of the culprits of this dangerous half-truth. Social media, text messages, and other digital connections provide just enough social interaction that we feel as though we are connected to other people. We can see their lives, experience their emotions (at least the ones they are willing to post online), and stay in touch with short notes or the compulsory "Happy Birthday" alert. The people we are "connected" with know we are here, and we know they are there. The obvious dilemma is that these relationships are only surface deep. We don't know what is really happening in their lives. Even when someone posts about a trial or adversity, we may not take the time to follow-up with a phone call or a personal visit because we've now been informed.

Even more, these platforms can erode our ability to gain the perspective of others. In the shallow waters of our social media circles, we bypass civil discourse and short-cut critical thinking, often only reinforcing our personal biases and beliefs or rejecting those in opposition. When we share news or information, the responses we receive, even the thoughtful ones, are limited to a lower form of human interaction—simple text—devoid of nuance, intonation, and the ability to discern or communicate intent.

The result is that not only do digital platforms provide a false sense of connection, but they can be a psychologically dangerous place where we are not able to seek meaningful connections, thoughtful advice, or true emotional care. Try publicly sharing about something you are struggling with or that you believe with conviction about the world. You'll tend to get binary replies, generic supportive, or unsupportive reactions. Most of your connections remain silent with few responses involving true questions or thoughtful inquiry. Not only can these digital connections be shallow, but they promote unrealistic social comparisons, eroding our leadership efficacy and leaving us feeling as though we are the only ones who are struggling, further perpetuating our sense of being alone.

I'm not saying that digital communication tools are wrong to use. They have a place, and they can, in fact, generate deeper connectivity to augment our actual relationships. It's amazing that I can connect so easily with my family members on the other side of the globe for spur of the moment video calls. I'm always delighted to catch up with a colleague in a different part of the world. As leaders, however, we fall victim to the false perception that we are connected without the real experience of a true relational investment. It's like a lingering scent or memory, something with a hint of meaning but not enough to last.

When the trials of leadership increase, distant and minimally attached relationships don't meet your deep-seated need for emotionally connected relationships. These relationships never met your needs in the first place; you just didn't realize the shallow depth till you come to face a need for greater levels of connection, only to find that your virtual life isn't congruent with the needs of the moment. When the sale of your business falls through at the last minute you need more than a text message from a friend.

Today, it's possible to "see" more people than ever, yet never know anyone deeply. The old irony of being alone in a crowd of people has taken a new form. We can believe that we are connected to a supportive network only to discover that not only are we alone in a crowd of people but that we are in fact just alone, perceiving that there are people around us when there aren't.

Digital connections can complement our relationships. As leaders, however, it's imperative that we stay consciously aware of our real needs for meaningful relationships and avoid getting stuck in a digital void, the empty calorie junk food of our relationships. Other people depend on us to be healthy and lead them well. Real, emotionally healthy relationships are a critical part of that.

Emotional Support Is a Core Psychological Need

Healthy, supportive relationships are considered a primary psychological need that is a key cornerstone to psychological and physical health. Because leading is an isolating activity, leaders need to know that they are cared for. Psychologists have demonstrated that we all need to be known and accepted and loved.[3] Leaders are no different. There is a reason that on average, individuals who are married and people who are active in a faith community tend to live longer, healthier, and happier lives.[4] The same goes for newborn babies who need physical touch and will fail to thrive without it.[5] Conversely, solitary confinement in prison systems is often considered the harshest punishment because it brings the emotional devastation of living without community and connection with other people.[6] Decades of research across different disciplines show this truth time and again. The fallacy of self-sufficiency, and the perception of connectedness, can be dangerous.

Whom can you turn to for this level of real, genuine connection? Often these people aren't inside your business. Past mentors, family members, and friends in other firms usually fill these invisible but foundational relational roles. When the pressure of leading rises, these relational investors can provide the platform for you to stand on.

The majority of CEOs I work with will confess that they have let close friendships and supportive community engagements fall away. People are busier than ever, and friendships are easy to deprioritize. But longevity requires connection. Friendships and social connections are one of the enduring themes for happy, healthy longevity across people and cultures.[7]

Regardless of whom you rely on, these are people who help you live into who you most truly are. They are people whom you can trust to provide you with unconditional positive regard and the safety to risk and grow. Knowing that we are supported allows us to have moments where we are alone as leaders, and yet not feel lonely. A circle of supportive relational investors reminds you of your purpose and meaningfulness of leading for something bigger than yourself. These are people whom you can confide in and who confirm your value and give you the gift of friendship and companionship.

Many of us have had these people in our lives at some point. The challenge is that we often lack the intentionality to foster those relationships as we go on our way. Like entropy and the tendency toward disorder, having support in the past doesn't mean that we still have it today. Like my parents, the gardeners in Chapter 3, we must continue to till and cultivate our relationships to reap the fruit and share it with other people. The good news is that by becoming more intentional with the relationships we already have, we begin to develop our ability to stay resilient and effective, for our sake and the sake of the people whom we are trusted to care for.

Relational investors who support you are especially important during moments of transition. Maybe you've taken a new job with a different organization, moved to a new community, or accepted a promotion. Leaders often find that the support systems they'd built in the past start to shift during these moments. Also, your developmental needs change during transitions and over time with your own levels of emotional maturity. It's OK to rely on someone for a season and not in the same ways for other seasons. Relationships are fluid. The nature of your relationships can look different over time. Taking regular inventory of who is supporting you can increase your resilience for the long term. You'll also begin to realize that you fill this role for other people in different ways. Tending our own relational gardens can increase our awareness of how we are supporting others who need what we may be able to provide.

Getting Real-Time Support

I've observed that leaders neglect cultivating emotionally supportive relational investors till it's too late. We don't realize the need for emotional support until it hits us. Quite simply, we don't get ready well. We don't always realize the need till we are in the moment. It's important to have those relationships in place before the storm hits. When acute emergencies or crises happen, the spike in pressure means that you will need to rely on other people in ways you never have before. Leaders who last for the long term realize that they will always need support throughout their lives.

Scott was a friend who provided me with real-time support in a very difficult season in my life and my work. Early in my career I'd experienced a few debilitating physical and mental health issues. My performance at work was suffering as a result and my social life and family relationships were impacted as well. I was at a low point. One day Scott gave me a call. He asked how I was doing. I wanted to share my struggles, but I didn't want to burden him. He kept asking questions. Finally, I cracked. I shared how I was struggling and the fear that I was experiencing.

Scott stepped up to support me in that season of life. He checked in on me regularly, encouraged me, and even challenged me to rise to the occasion when I needed to. Scott didn't try to solve my problems; he was just there to connect with me.[8] He went with me in my journey to recover my health and well-being. I didn't need an advisor or mentor in this situation. I needed someone to encourage me and remind me that things would change for the better. I knew that I could call Scott just to share how I was doing. He'd join me for a walk and just listen to me and ask me questions.

Eventually my health improved, and my life and work were in a better place. The support that Scott offered me was critical in enduring that season of life. It was difficult to accept his support at first but I'm so grateful that I had a friend step up to care for me when I needed it the most.

Asking for Help Takes Intentionality and Humility

Some leaders don't have a lot of relational investors whom they can rely on for emotional support. But most of the leaders I've worked with do have people around them. The challenge is that we often don't think that people are willing to help, or we just don't ask. Adversity can emotionally flood you, causing your perspective to shrink. This makes it difficult to see the relational investors around you who are ready and willing to listen without judgement and remind you that you aren't leading alone.

Getting emotional support takes tremendous humility. To combat the fallacies that we believe about ourselves requires us to step out and ask for help. Interestingly, asking for help can give others psychological permission to seek help themselves. By role modeling appropriate vulnerability and guarding ourselves from isolation we can show other leaders the better and healthier way, causing a positive domino effect.

Asking for help takes intentionality and humility. Intentionality is required because we need to be purposeful. Unlike your favorite social media platform, you don't need hundreds of followers. The emotional support part of your circle of relational investors is about quality over mere quantity. The research suggests that having a core group of just a few people is all that is needed to provide the powerful buffering effect that allows you to weather stress and chaos.[9] Nearly every leader I've worked with has this short list at their fingertips, often they just haven't taken a first step to activate the support that is waiting for them.

Humility is needed because we must acknowledge that we don't have all the resources we need. We are not self-sufficient. No individual leader can carry all the weight of a family, a team, or an organization on their own. Case studies of hero leaders make great books and movies, but they blind us to the reality that leaders are people too. To ignore your humanity takes a selective view on the beauty and brokenness that you have as a leader. Leading creates the conditions that can make us aware of our limits. Necessities such as sleep, food, and water are monotonous daily reminders of our boundaries and constraints. No leader, regardless of experience or pedigree, has risen above the need for daily sustenance.

On the contrary, there is a paradoxical freedom in our constraints in life and leadership. Recognizing and then embracing our limitations opens the opportunity to rely on others, providing them an opportunity to exercise their talent and wisdom. Ironically, embracing limitations and the need for emotional support can increase the reach and scale of a leader.

In many ways, effective leadership is about growing in our own maturity as a person. It's true that it takes a village to raise (and sustain) a leader for the long term. By surrounding ourselves with relational investors that allow us to grow in our maturity, we create strength for the present and resiliency for the future. This matters for you but also for the individuals whom you lead. Getting surrounded with emotional support can feel self-centered but nothing could be further from the truth. Your levels of support have a trickle-down effect on the people you lead and influence. Responsible leaders run away from the recklessness of isolation, abandon the hero complex, and surround themselves with support.

Reflection Questions

- Who is relationally surrounding you right now with support and care? Whom do you feel safe to take emotional or relational risks with?
- What would change if you had greater levels of meaningful connection?

> - How is your ability to invest in others connected to the circle of support that is surrounding you?
> - What helps or hinders your ability to build deep relationships of support?
> - What is one step you can take today to foster deeper emotional support?

Take Action: Make a Plan to Ask for Help

When the storms of life hit you, you need relationships to help anchor you. Asking for help can be difficult if you feel overwhelmed. Start by identifying two or three people whom you can reach out to for support. Then create a simple plan to connect with them. Write down the names of two or three people whom you can rely on to process what you are thinking, what you are feeling, and how you are behaving. This simple exercise could be the difference maker for your leadership effectiveness.

- *Who* comes to mind?

    1. ___________________________________

    2. ___________________________________

    3. ___________________________________

- *When* will you reach out them?

    ____

- *How* will you initiate the connection?

    ____

- *What* are you going to ask them to help you with?

    ____

7 | Mentors: The Magic of Mentoring

Key Takeaways

- Mentors are people who have gone before you and are willing to share wisdom, insights, and advice from the journey they've been on.

- Mentors bring three key benefits: (1) expert guidance that accelerates your growth, (2) life support to help you navigate your personal and professional twists and turns, and (3) role modeling by showing you the pathway to success so that you can follow in their footsteps.

- If you are an emerging leader, your manager can become a great mentor but not all managers are equipped to mentor you. Valuable mentoring can come from your manager, a leader on another team, or a leader outside your organization.

- Three keys for making the most out of your mentoring relationships are: (1) specificity about your needs, (2) clear expectations, and (3) making yourself "mentorable."

- As relational investors mentor you, you'll become inspired to consider how you can become that type of mentor in someone else's circle of relational investors.

There is something magical about mentoring. Mentors are the most widely known relational investor role with the deepest research. Relational investors grow your leadership capacity by stretching you, supporting you, and being strategic for you. When it comes to support, mentoring is a leading role in your trust circle. Mentors are people who have gone before you and are willing to share wisdom, insights, and advice from the journey they've been on. Sometimes mentors support you in very specific ways for very specific seasons of life. Other mentors provide a broader base of support, filling a range of relational roles, with the investment they make in you evolving over time as you mature.[1]

In this chapter, we will learn about the benefits of having a mentor in your circle of relational investors and look at how to gain the most from your mentoring relationships. Like every chapter, we will also consider how you can become the relational investor for someone else's circle as well.

The Power of Mentoring

I was in the middle of leading a high-stakes offsite for a client when mentoring became meaningful. This was a business with some of the smartest technologists and inventors in the world. They'd received significant early funding for an innovation platform, but they were at a critical juncture.

After merging three organizations together, their path to success was blocked by the sticky work of blending cultures and aligning leaders in the same direction. A mix of conflict, fear, and ego threatened to undo their work and prevent them from pursuing and acquiring capital as a unified front. I was asked to facilitate a critical conversation about the current realities and future direction. It was a make it or break it moment for this business.

If you've ever facilitated a high-stakes offsite strategy session or mediated a conflict management intervention, then you know these moments are emotionally intense. Toward the end of day two, I was starting to run on empty. As we finished the day, a well-dressed man strolled into the conference room. I didn't recognize him, but he seemed to know the leadership team. His name was Graeme Weston, and it turns out that he was the chair of the board.

Graeme had stopped in to get a sense for how the discussions had gone. He warmly introduced himself to me and asked if I was the facilitator for the event. He let me know that he'd heard very good things about the session, the productive conversations we'd had, and the amount of ground we had covered in a short time. I was happy to hear that because I was ready to take a nap.

Then Graeme surprised me by asking me a question that I had received often as a younger leader. Well, to be fair, it was less of a question and more of a statement: "You look really young; tell me, how is someone at your age able to so effectively lead a session like this with such a seasoned group of leaders?"

Normally I'm careful and measured with my words but I was tired. This time I just blurted out my response: "Over the years I've had dozens of people mentor me and disproportionately invest in me as a leader for reasons that I still am trying to figure out. But it's because of that disproportionate investment that I've been able to accelerate certain capabilities, like the ability to facilitate an offsite like this." He smiled, gave me his business card, and told me that we should stay in touch as we'd be working together again.

I turned around laughing to myself for two reasons; first, I don't normally have such a quick response, and second, it instantly made me think of the dozens of relational investors who had mentored me over the years. The reason I could facilitate that offsite was because of the investment of mentors. I could immediately identify the names of relational investors who taught me the skills I needed and gave me the confidence to deliver. Mentoring brings magic to your career.

Years later, when I interviewed Graeme for this book, he shared a paradox he learned as a leader: we need people and their support and guidance, and ultimately, we must take responsibility for the direction of our lives and leadership and find our own way. He read me a letter that a mentor of his had given him when he was a young man, starting his career. It perfectly captures the tension of learning from others and figuring it out for yourself.

> "Dear Graeme,
>
> My affectionate good wishes on your birthday. What a glorious age for one of your intelligence and character. Life, a vessel to be filled with love and work, with achievement and challenge, with friendship and development. And how fortunate you are to have the intelligence and dominance to fill that vessel with beauty and service. Do not be alarmed that you cannot see into the future, nor chastise yourself about your own uncertainties. These are a part of youth and life is far more dull if all is certain than when the unknown is before you with both its challenges and rewards. But even at your age, there are guide stars we can seek for ourselves, perhaps to contribute to the life betterment of less advantaged, to serve your community as well as yourself, to cherish your integrity as something once lost cannot be regained, and to know that what is excellent does not come easily. Ah, I am full of admonitions. Think through your own and be guided by them. Goethe once said, beware of what you ask in your youth for in your old age, you will have it. Be well and be confident. The future is indeed yours."

Mentoring Makes the Difference

If you are preparing a successor for your role then helping your successor find mentors outside of your business and even industry can be an invaluable source of wisdom and guidance. If you are that rising leader who is being developed to run a business, then mentors can be the key to accelerate your growth.

The concept of mentoring has been around for centuries. The roots of mentoring can be traced back to Greek mythology.[2]

Mentoring has become commonplace for leaders. "How do I find a mentor?" is a question that's asked across college campuses and in virtually every type of organization.

There are hundreds of books, articles, videos, and guides on how to find a mentor, how to become a mentor, or how to build a mentoring program that develops talent in organizations. Mentoring gets attention for good reason. It's clear from the research that people who have mentors are happier, more confident, perform better, get paid more, and are promoted more often.[3] Who wouldn't want a mentor?

The experience of countless leaders affirms what the research shows. Mentoring works to develop people and leaders. So how do you make mentoring work for you? That's the key question in this chapter. We'll look at the unique value that mentors bring. Then, we'll explore how to know when you need a mentor and what type of person you should look for in a mentor. Lastly, we'll look at the secrets to making mentoring work so that you can lead for the long term.

Let's start with the value of mentoring. The mentoring research highlights three key benefits that effective mentors bring: (1) expert guidance that accelerates your growth, (2) life support to help you navigate your personal and professional twists and turns, and (3) role modeling by showing you the pathway to success so that you can follow in their footsteps.

Expert Guidance

Matt's expert guidance took my professional development to a new level. At the age of 23, I was convinced that I was going to become an executive career coach. The glaring problem was my age. Every executive coach who I met told me that I was far too young to be a career coach. One leader briskly told me that I needed at least 10 years of experience in human resources before I'd be able to provide any value to a leader. Another executive of a firm on my wish list candidly told me that no one on his staff was younger than the age of 40. I was deflated after these calls.

Then I heard of Matt Youngquist, one of the top executive career coaches in the Pacific Northwest. His name came up everywhere. It seemed as if every executive I was meeting had used Matt's services. One day my future father-in-law started working with Matt. He called me after a workshop he'd attended and told me that I had to meet Matt. He made an introduction and I acted quickly to set up a meeting over coffee. I wanted to get advice on how to break into the career coaching field and get established. Before we met, I did my research. I was ready with questions to take the conversation beyond the typical meet and greet.

When Matt and I met, he described his work and shared how tough it was to break in without significant experience as a leader. I'd heard this line before. But Matt also told me a different story. After we discussed the challenge of my age, he also told me that he started this work when he was 23 as well. Two decades later he was the go-to coach for executives in career transition. Matt confirmed that it was true—the front door to the industry was through executive leadership or by getting that decade of human resources and a few certifications. But Matt also showed me the secret back door entrance to the industry. This gave me hope.

Matt appreciated that I had come ready to engage at a deeper level, so he offered to meet again. I brought as many questions as I could about the field. I wanted to know everything. Over the next eight years, I met with Matt regularly, always bringing new, thoughtful questions so that I could learn the details of the profession. If Matt suggested a book, I'd buy it immediately. If there was a training or workshop or opportunity to learn, I'd prioritize it. If he gave me a strategy for working with a client, I'd put it to practice right away.

Matt helped to connect me with dozens of his peers so that they could expand my network. As my skills grew, he referred countless young professional clients to me. Words can't express the investment he made in me and how that generous gift of time, energy, and skill helped me to hone my craft and establish myself.

When I landed a coveted job in a career counseling center, I realized that I'd won the role over people with significantly more experience than I had. That accomplishment was largely because of the abilities I'd developed from Matt's mentoring. To say that the trajectory of my career was influenced by Matt would be an understatement.

Matt's influence on me is on display in Chapter 8 of this book on the importance of career connection and how to navigate leadership career transitions. What I learned from Matt in those early years was foundational in influencing the way that I serve leaders today. Now, years after I first met Matt, I have the honor of referring executives to him for career counseling, job search coaching, or résumé writing.

One of the most powerful advantages of having a mentor is expert guidance. Do you have someone like Matt who is willing to teach you a new profession or how to lead at a different level? Expert guidance is irreplaceable in your circle of relational investors.

Life Support

Mentors are an incredible source of expert guidance, but sometimes what you need is life support to navigate personal challenges. Steve Poole was a mentor who supported me in a tough season of life that was full of change. Steve met with me every other week and offered wisdom, insights, and encouragement in life.

Steve's support was primarily personal and spiritual. We attended the same church, and our values were closely aligned. Steve's investment in me helped me grow as a leader by supporting the personal and family sides of my life. Steve had the type of character that I wanted to emulate. Steve's life had stood the test of time. He'd raised a great family and was a model for the type of husband and father I aspired to become. Steve's influence in my life grew when I started dating my future wife.

When Kristin and I were engaged, Steve and his wife, Julie, both mentored us as a couple. Their relationship guided our blossoming relationship during a very stressful season of planning for a wedding, preparing for marriage, and establishing ourselves in our careers to get ready for having a family.

Steve and Julie's investment in us was meaningful and perfectly timed for us. Professionally, Steve's career focus was different from mine and while work related issues came up in our conversations, it wasn't the focus of our time together. The impact of the investment that Steve and Julie made is still alive today. They helped to set us on the trajectory to be leaders who last, starting in our marriage. Sometimes, the most meaningful investment from mentors is life support.

Role Modeling

Even though most leaders know that mentoring matters, there are lots of barriers to getting the mentoring that we often need. One barrier to mentoring is that the term mentor sometimes carries a heavy weight. "Will you be my mentor?" can feel like asking a leader to adopt you into their family and write you into their will. Mentors also often feel tremendous responsibility for their role as mentor, and they can feel guilty if they can't provide what they perceive that you as their mentee needs.

Just because you haven't had the "mentor me" talk, doesn't mean you aren't getting meaningful mentoring. There is no rule that says a mentor needs to be as invested as Matt was with me or get as personal as Steve and Julie did for my wife and me. Deep mentoring relationships like those are special, but they aren't always the norm. Sometimes, a meaningful mentoring relationship won't ever have the title of "mentor" associated with it. Many mentors serve as role models, giving you an example to watch and emulate. In the mentoring research role modeling was one of the strongest predictors of positive career outcomes.[4]

Lacey is a senior leader who has mentored dozens of leaders into executive roles. She has been a role model for countless more. Her deep business experience provides her with the specific experiences to pass on to rising leaders in her business. She knows what they should expect and can help them navigate pitfalls and opportunities, guiding them to make critical decisions for their career or providing very practical advice on how to approach the work. Rising leaders who work with Lacey can learn from her experience but also by watching how she carries herself as an executive who adds value to the organizations that she serves.

Many leaders have even described role modeling from historical figures and biographies. Graeme Weston from the beginning of this chapter told me about a personal crisis he faced during a moment in life when his business at the time collapsed, he lost a loved one, and he underwent immense personal stress and couldn't sleep well for a year. He described it as the first time in his life that he couldn't see the horizon. He found inspiration in the stories of George Washington and Winston Churchill. But he didn't look to them for a prescription; he looked at them for hope and to see how to overcome the impossible. Churchill's famous words, "When you're going through hell, keep going." echoed for him. He learned that storms are inevitable but that what matters is what you do with them.

When leaders have someone to emulate or to inspire them, it can boost confidence and buffer the feelings of loneliness that can hinder their ability to lead effectively.[5] A role model whom you watch, or a simple mentoring moment can provide the example you need to see to give you a picture of "how it's done" so that you can act on your own. As you build your circle, some of the most powerful relational investments you receive will simply be role models whom you can watch and learn from or draft inspiration from to find your own path.

Is Mentoring What You Need?

Mentors are a crucial part of your circle of relational investors. I've spoken to many leaders who'd love to have a mentor, but they haven't taken the steps to get one. Other leaders have mentors in place, but they aren't accessing the full range of benefits that their mentor is ready to provide. Before you approach another leader for mentorship, ask yourself these questions:

- Why do you want a mentor?
- What do you hope to learn from your mentor?
- What difference could a mentor make for you as a leader? How would that impact other people around you?

Your answers to these questions might reveal that mentoring isn't what you most need in this season of your life. Maybe what you really need is someone to provide you with honest feedback (read Chapter 3), or possibly you really need an advocate to open opportunities for you (read Chapter 10). If the support of a mentor is what you need the most, then why? Are you hoping for someone to help you accelerate your career by providing you insights from their journey and their experiences? Do you need someone to support you as you navigate major life transitions? Are you looking for role models whom you can watch and learn from?

Knowing what you hope to gain from a mentor will build your circle of relational investors and help you discern whom to approach for mentorship. Do you need to sit with a mentor who's already sold their business or successfully passed it to the next generation? What was the process like? What lessons can you learn? What mistakes should you avoid? How long should you stay around and when should you go? These are questions where a mentor who has gone ahead of you can provide insights. The more clarity you have about what you want in a mentor, the more you'll benefit from the relationship and the more rewarding it will be for your mentor too.[6] Mentors want to know that they are serving you with valuable help and insights. Some of your mentors will come from likely places, but some might be unexpected.[7]

Mentoring from Your Manager

When I ask leaders about the people who have invested in them as mentors, many will share about a manager who went beyond supervising their work. Almost every leader has worked for a bad role model or an ineffective manager. If you are an emerging leader, the person you report to has the potential to impact your work more than any other working relationship. Direct managers who are effective people developers can accelerate your growth. The leader you report to is one of the best sources of direct, first-hand feedback, advocacy, and coaching. Over time they can learn your strengths and blind spots, targeting your growth and helping you point your career in the right direction.

After completing my PhD I was looking for my next career opportunity. Dave Gartenberg, a mentoring voice, wisely encouraged me to prioritize looking for people I wanted to work with instead of only targeting interesting organizations. His point was that the leader you report to is in an important and influential position to invest in you and help you grow. Not every inspiring leader is effective at mentoring and developing people. This mentor was that type of person, so I valued his input. At the end of our conversation, I asked him for the names of 10 leaders whom he'd want to work for. He advocated for me to those leaders and one of them hired me for a developmentally rich role. Dave continued to serve as a mentor for me alongside the mentoring from my new direct manager.

Managers can become great mentors, but not all managers are equipped to mentor you in the ways that you need. Sometimes your manager will be a rich source of development, but not always. Valuable mentoring can come from inside your organization, from your manager, or a leader on another team. It can come from a leader outside your organization. This takes the pressure off your mentor to meet all your developmental needs, and it decreases the developmental pressure you place on any single mentor.[8]

Megan Lawrence, a leader on my team, needed expert guidance in an area of our business that I wasn't a specialist. I was able to ask thoughtful questions to encourage or challenge her but there was a level of technical specificity that she needed and that I couldn't provide. At the same time, I was having a conversation with my friend Derek Gillette, a leader who happened to be an expert in solving the business problems that Megan was responsible for. I connected them and Megan was able to share ideas with Derek and get his input on some of the projects she was working on. In the process, I was able to learn from Megan as she learned from Derek.

Even 20 years into my career, mentoring matters. When I became a partner at The Sage Group®, I knew that I had a lot to learn from our founding partner and managing director, Ron Worman. What I didn't realize was how much I'd grow under his mentorship and how much I'd learn. I've told friends that working with Ron as my mentor has been more developmental than both of my graduate degrees. A mentor on the job can accelerate the velocity of your growth.

Great managers often continue to mentor leaders who have worked for them, long after those leaders move on to their next assignment. Your relationship with your manager can continue to evolve over time. Your mentor might even work for you one day.

Similar or Different?

Mentoring comes in different forms. Some mentors will be like you, just farther along in their journey, others will be unlikely mentors who are very different from what you'd expect in a mentor. Some mentors will emerge from informal relationships and others from formal mentoring programs.[9] Your mentor could be a peer or your manager. Some mentors are for a very brief season and a very specific reason. Other mentors are life-long relationships that mature and develop over time. Wherever you find mentoring, once you know why you want a mentor you will be more prepared to learn as much as you can.

It's easy to look for a leader who has a similar journey to yours, someone who was trained in the same discipline or who ran a business in the same industry. Many leaders are surprised, however, when they find that a mentor who has an unexpected background can spur creative thinking. When it comes to selecting a mentor or making the most out of a mentoring relationship, sometimes the unlikely mentor can provide the most unexpected value.

Consider finding a mentor who sees the world differently than you. Who has a radically different life experience than you? What might they offer you that you haven't realized? Chemistry and connection are important for mentors but often leaders find themselves surrounded with people just like them. The process of development is a process of change. Sometimes an unlikely mentor can provide unexpected value by changing your perspective.

The same goes for investing in unlikely leaders. Who are the unlikely leaders around you? What can you provide them as a mentor? As you build relationships that support you, you'll find yourself increasingly in the position to provide support to others.

The gift of mentoring creates the responsibility and opportunity to steward your relational and social capital to invest in the development of other leaders. Mentoring is an on-ramp to the highway of opportunity that is created by social and relational capital. The more mentoring you receive, the more you have to offer to other leaders as well. Relational investors give to you so that you can become a relational investor who gives to others.

Making Mentoring Work

Whether your mentors are like you or different from you depends on your goals and the type of support that you need. Regardless of how similar you are to your mentor, the relationship works better when you take initiative to start the relationship, set the expectations, and continue to come prepared to learn from your mentor. The responsibility to foster the relationship rests on you.

I'm obsessed with delicious fresh squeezed orange juice. It doesn't take a lot of work to squeeze juice at first. Just cut the orange in half and press it into the machine. Getting all the juice takes more work. Most of the orange peels will still have fruit after you juice them. Mentoring relationships are much like making fresh orange juice; you get as much out of the relationship as you want to squeeze. When it comes to making mentoring work, the relationship is in your hands. Three keys for making the most out of your mentoring relationships are specificity, clear expectations, and making yourself "mentorable."

The Power of Specificity

Specificity is one of the main ingredients for intentional development as a leader. You'll get as much out of a mentoring relationship as you put in. Initiative with specificity creates learning. Without specificity, mentoring relationships will lack actionable purpose.

If you and your mentor have great rapport, then you'll both enjoy your conversations, but a vague and undefined purpose will lead to vague and unfulfilled outcomes. It's hard to get specific about what you need. When I coach leaders, I work to challenge them to move from vague aspirations or ideas into specific beliefs or actions that they can influence. Most leaders squirm a bit when I push them to get specific about what they need. Specificity puts us to the edge of our comfort zone. It creates clarity and forces us to commit to act. Specificity turns aspirations into actions.

What do you want from your mentor? The more clarity that you can communicate to your mentor, the more intentionality that they will be able to bring to your relationship. This closes the gap between where you are now and where you want to be next. Your specificity activates your mentor's intentionality.

Setting Clear Expectations

Specificity is powerful for any development relationship in your circle, especially your mentors. Knowing what you want starts with intentionality. Communicating what you want makes it real. Your mentor wants to serve you but needs your help to know how. How often do you want to meet with your mentor? What are you hoping to learn from them? Where do you need expert guidance, life support, or role modeling? When you meet with your mentor, plan the agenda ahead of time. State your intent for the conversation at the outset, either in a note ahead of time, or at the start of your conversation. "Thanks so much for making time this week, I'm always grateful for your wisdom. Today I'm hoping to get your perspective on____."

Depending on the nature of your mentoring relationship you might co-create the agenda with your mentor. "I'm not quite sure what to do next, I'd really like your guidance on what I should be focusing on right now." You might disagree with one of your mentors, and that's OK too. You don't have to do everything your mentor suggests: "That's a different perspective than mine. I value that you challenge my assumptions. I think I need to process that a bit more. I'll do some reflection and let you know what I'm thinking."

Whether you communicate the outcome you want or identify a shared agenda together, it's up to you to drive the relationship. You are primarily responsible for setting the agenda and following up.

One mentor of mine was investing in several leaders. He told me that he would meet with me as often as I needed on any topic he could help with. He only asked that I let him know how he could serve me best so that we could make the most out of our time together.

Becoming "Mentorable"

There is nothing more rewarding to a mentor than to see a mentee learn, grow, and succeed. Mentors get tremendous personal value out of sharing their wisdom or expertise, especially if they can see that investing in you will have an impact on other people. I was mentored for a year by another Matt, Matt Groshong, the Dean of Students in a college that I worked in. We got to know each other through mutual work on a committee. I resonated with the level of integrity he demonstrated in the way he carried himself and made decisions. I reached out to have a conversation with him to learn more about his approach to leadership. My initiative caught his interest, and he told me that he'd be happy to mentor me if I'd find value in meeting periodically. I took him up on it. After a few months I became curious about why he was investing in me. He told me that he could tell that investing in me would equip me to invest in others. In fact, he expected it. When I left the institution for another role, he challenged me to continue to pour into other people like he had poured into me.

If you are an emerging leader who plans to grow into ownership or executive leadership then it's important to mentors that you are worth the investment of their energy. Showing yourself to be "mentorable" encourages relational investors to spend time with you, knowing that their efforts will go to good use. Being a mentorable leader means that you demonstrate a hunger to learn, a readiness to put your learning into action, and a desire to grow in effectiveness for your sake, but also for the sake of others.

It's the intangibles that make you mentorable. Careful preparation, thoughtful questions, and diligent follow-up demonstrate over time that you are a sure bet for mentoring. Mentors will invest in you over time as your put their investments to work. By making yourself mentorable, other leaders will see the value in supporting you. This puts you in a greater position to do that for other leaders in the future, now and for the long term. After all, becoming a leader who lasts is about taking what you receive and finding ways to give to others. Make yourself mentorable so that you can more effectively mentor other leaders.

Moving on from a Mentor

A core theme of this book is that you need different relationships for different reasons and in different seasons. The beauty of developmental relationships is that the people who surround you can change over time and the ways that they pour into you, and you pour into them, will evolve over time. Some mentoring relationships deepen and change from a focus on technical proficiency to more personal and purposeful. Many mentors and mentees meet for years. Some mentoring relationships are very specific for a defined period. This means that it's OK for you to meet with a mentor more intentionally for a season of time and then to shift that relationship over time.

Back to that intentional manager who supports you and develops you. If you leave the organization, it's likely that they won't have the capacity to invest in you to the same level as when you were on their team. That doesn't mean you can't stay in touch and connect periodically or just-in-time if you had a critical moment where you wanted their input. Relationships naturally shift over time. By bringing intentionality with specificity, you'll know what you need in this season of your development, and you'll be able to discern who can support you in that way.

Giving, Receiving, and Giving Again

Mentoring relationships have the power to shape your life. My mentoring experiences with Matt, Steve, and Julie, and others are just a glimpse into the influence that mentors can have on your development, personally and professionally. As relational investors mentor you, you'll become inspired to consider how you can become that type of mentor for someone else. Continue to pour into other leaders from the overflow of what you've been given. Mentors are a pivotal part of your system of leader support.

Throughout this book, I've been encouraging you to get intentional and specific about the type of support you need as a leader. Asking for support doesn't always feel natural and sometimes we don't want to inconvenience other busy leaders by asking them to stop and invest in us. Hopefully, you're already seeing how developing intentional relationships don't have to feel instrumental or exploitive. When done well, the best mentoring relationships will be marked by gratitude and mutual generosity that goes beyond reciprocity. You can give back to your mentors with gratitude and reverse mentoring.

Most mentors will say that investing in you is more rewarding for them than it is for you. Asking a mentor for help or advice signals that they are valuable and have something to offer. Sharing their journey and giving you advice makes their own struggles and trials meaningful and worthwhile. The intrinsic reward that mentors receive is beyond description and your gratitude and development is what most mentors are looking for. It feels good to give to others, especially if they take your input and turn it into action.[10]

Many mentors will even tell you that they feel like they are getting more out of the mentorship than you are as a mentee. Mentoring is multidirectional and reverse mentoring also occurs as your relationship develops. Leaders in senior roles have shared with me what they learned from mentoring emerging leaders. Al Erisman is a semi-retired executive who focuses his time on writing, speaking, and investing in and actively mentoring other leaders. He told me that at his life stage there were very few leaders left to mentor him. He is now getting reverse mentoring. He is continually challenged to learn and grow and stay sharp by the younger leaders he was investing in. They call him their mentor, and he calls them that too.

Mentoring Pays Off

Expert guidance, life support, and role modeling are the reasons why mentors make the difference in your career success. The fun part of mentoring is the relationships that develop over the long term. In the moment it might feel like your mentor is doing all the giving and you are the only one gaining, but over time you'll find ways to serve them as well. In Chapter 3 I mentioned Jeff Rogers, one of the business leaders who helped change my perspective on professional relationships. After several years of meaningful investments in me, Jeff's daughter, Lauren became one of the graduate business students in my care.

Lauren was full of energy, and I enjoyed being a part of her professional development and in helping launch her as a leader. In my mind it was just part of my job; I loved working with my students. But Jeff made it a point to thank me, letting me know that he couldn't fully express his gratitude for supporting his daughter. He told me that as my kids grew that I'd see how priceless it is when someone pours into your kids.

It was so much fun to be able to serve Jeff through Lauren in a meaningful way as he'd given so much to me. The number of ways that you can serve the mentoring voices in your life is limited simply by your imagination. As you receive the gift of mentoring, keep your eyes open for the range of ways that you can bless your mentors, now or in the future. Today, Lauren is flourishing in her career and I'm honored that I was able to play a small part in it, just as her father was able to for me.

Mentoring matters. When done with intention, the support of a constellation of mentors can help you grow and develop in rich and deep ways, accelerating your effectiveness, supporting you through the ups and downs of life and work, and modeling potential pathways for healthy leadership. As you receive the gift of mentoring, it will sharpen your ability to mentor others, giving to them from what you have received.

> **Reflection Questions**
>
> - What type of mentoring is most important for you at this moment in time? Why? (*Expert Guidance, Life Support, or Role Modeling?*)
> - Fill in the blank: "I need a mentoring voice to help me _________?"
> - Why would another leader want to mentor you? How will an investment in you equip you to serve other people?
> - What can you prepare today to get ready for your next mentor tomorrow?
> - Whom are you in a position to mentor and invest in?

Take Action

Deepen Your Existing Mentoring Relationships

- Reflect on your current or past mentoring relationships. For each relationship, identify at least one specific area where this person has helped you to grow.
- Reach out to them to express your gratitude for their investment in your development.

Prepare to Invest in Others

- Identify 2–3 people whom you could see yourself mentoring in the future.
- For each person, identify at least one specific area of expertise or insight that you could offer them.
- Set up time to meet with each of them to begin building a mentoring relationship.

Strategy

Strategic relationships are indispensable for leaders—research and common sense support that. The challenge is that the idea of relationships that are strategic can sound cold and calculated. Many of us have experienced a leader who treated people like pawns on a chessboard, disposable resources to reach their own goals. The reality is that you need strategic relationships to be effective in your role, to move to your next level of capability, and to help elevate the people that you lead. The good news is that strategic relationships don't need to be soulless. Taking an others-oriented approach, marked by generosity and mutuality, can transform your strategic relationships beyond mere instrumentality and goal acquisition.

Meaningful strategic relationships help you position yourself to take advantage of future opportunities, for yourself and others in your care. Savvy, caring leaders build trusting, strategic relationships for their own sake but also for the sake of the people whom they are called to care for. Few leaders can take advantage of the full range of their social capital. A leader with a wealth of strategic relationships has the opportunity and responsibility to use their excess relational equity to serve the people whom they lead.

Leaders need relationships that stretch them to grow and relationships that support them in times of need to weather storms.

Your strategic relationships position you for influence, growth, and increased opportunities to use your gifts to serve others.

In this part, we'll focus on the importance of external networks of career connections who can help you transition to new opportunities (Chapter 8) and the importance of advocates who create access to opportunities (Chapter 9).

Many leaders neglect to foster networks of external career connections until they are suddenly in between roles, struggling to know where to turn. In a dynamic and changing world, having relationships outside of your organization can be the difference for preserving career continuity and successfully navigating the difficult transitions that are inevitable. Strong career networks also embolden you to take strategic risks, knowing that you aren't solely depending on your current role for financial provision.

Advocates are a special strategic relationship that creates opportunities for you. Advocates use their social capital on your behalf, opening doors for you, breaking down doors that you can't get into, or creating doors where it seems that none exist. Advocates put their reputation on the line for you and propel you to places you'd never be able to reach on your own.

Building leadership agility requires that we have strategic relationships with people who can help connect us to future opportunities to serve others as well as to people who will create opportunities for us to serve others. Let's get surrounded by people who strategically position us for our sake and for the sake of the people we are responsible for caring for.

8
Career Connections: The Inside Track

Key Takeaways

- Career transitions carry the greatest risk for career derailment. Your career connections are about the relational investors you would call tomorrow if you were looking for a job.
- People switch jobs every five years or less, creating for the potential of 8–10 major role transitions over your lifetime.
- The bad news: transitions are challenging. Most leaders aren't quite prepared to shift jobs. They are forced to get ready in real time. The good news: there is always someone who is looking for your skills, you just need to learn how to find them. Your circle of relational investors can help.
- The "hidden" job market is where people with a career connection learn about a job opening before it's posted for the public. This is the inside track. Your trust circle can help discover your value, define your value, distribute your value, and deliver your value.

- Strong career connections help you stay engaged in your current role. Even if you don't plan to leave, knowing that you have the options to take a calculated risk gives you the opportunity to be at your best.

Yesterday you were essential, today you are expendable, tomorrow is ambiguous. One of the most unsettling events that leaders deal with in their careers are times of transition. It could be the tiresome work of climbing the proverbial ladder, one rung at a time. Maybe it's the story of returning to work after a season of investing in children or caring for an aging family. For others it's the boom and bust of entrepreneurship. You will leave your organization at some point. It might be due to a reorganization, a downsizing, an acquisition or merger, or a new top leader coming in and bringing in a new team. Everyone transitions out of the company at some point, even the owner will someday retire, die, or pass on the business to the next generation. No matter the reason, moments of transition carry greatest risk for derailment in your career. Your strategic career connections are your most important relational investors when it's time to transition to a new role.

In this chapter, we'll get ready for the unexpected by investing in a critical part of your circle of relational investors, the career connections who help you make strategic moves. This chapter is especially written for the CEO or senior executive who doesn't own the business but is stewarding it for another person or a group of shareholders. Transitions like the scale, sale, or succession of a business can cause you to suddenly find yourself on the job market without much warning. If you are the owner or the future owner of the business, this chapter will give you insights into the mind of the key leaders on your team as they consider their careers and how their goals align with yours. Pay attention so that you can retain your most important talent.

We'll start by looking at the gritty reality of making a transition when you've been caught off guard and the potential risks of drifting toward career derailment. We'll look at building career connections that help you get ready for the unexpected and consider how your network can help you take a calculated risk. We'll also see how your circle of relational investors can position you to get the inside track on new opportunities. You'll finish this chapter by answering the question, "Who would you call tomorrow if you're suddenly looking for a job?"

Caught by Surprise

For many leaders, the story line goes something like this—you start to grow in responsibility and increasing success, the greater your success the greater the reward—along with further responsibility. Work becomes an increased priority for you. You focus more intently. Between work and the rest of life with family or community involvement, you become singularly focused on getting things done. You keep leading forward but one day you find yourself on the market—either by force or by choice—only to discover that while you were laser focused on your role that you'd neglected to build or foster the relationships that you need to navigate the complexities of the modern job market. You are caught by surprise.

Eric experienced this firsthand. After 29 years in the same food manufacturer and distributor, Eric was planning to work 5 more years, retiring early at the age of 60. He'd worked his way up through the business over the years through multiple positions from driving a truck, to eventually managing a plant before taking over the second in command role as Vice President of Operations and Distribution. He knew the business inside and out and had great relationships throughout the organization.

To his shock, one day he was let go without much warning. A disagreement with the president of the firm resulted in his termination. He was caught off guard and said that the news felt like "a punch to the gut." His long-time commitment and dedication to the organization didn't matter. Getting out on the market was hard and not just because it had been so long since he'd had to run a professional job search. At his level, there were very few roles in his industry.

His world was full of new questions. Should he play the long game and find the "right" role? Should he compromise and take something just to stop the ticking clock—getting off unemployment and saving the severance package that was quickly running out? When he did try to compete for roles a step below his last position, he was told that he was overqualified, repeatedly. Maybe it was time to look at adjacent industries. The trouble here was that the companies he met with had a hard time translating his experience into the needs of their business. Transferable skills are a real thing, especially in the case of leading, but employers want plug and play if they can. Spending time to bring a new leader up to speed on the industry or sector is costly. Some firms will make the investment, many won't.

After nearly a year of transition, Eric landed a job with a startup that was selling a new product to the industry he'd grown up in. Over the next 10 years, Eric would find himself in 4 more roles with different firms, an average of one every 2–3 years. He'd have to exercise his career network muscles multiple times, including another gap that lasted nearly a year. For someone who'd put close to 30 years into one company, transitions quickly became the norm.

A story like Eric's is the reason that your career connections matter—and his journey isn't unique. I've seen it many times. Hard work and commitment are essential ingredients to success but it's the seemingly unexpected moments that test our preparation. After all, few of us plan for our employer to go out of business or for the product or service we support to lose ground in the market. No leader plans for their largest donor to diversify their giving or for the demographics of their market to shift overnight.

Drifting Toward Derailment

Transitions often surprise leaders. If you aren't ready, then being in transition can make you feel adrift. Yesterday you had a mission, a budget, and a team. You felt productive and effective. You were an integral part of something bigger than yourself. People depended on you.

Today, you are struggling to stay motivated in your career hunt. Putting in a "full day's work" in your search is a struggle. You don't have the systems and structures in place you relied on before and you don't have any accountability or community, upward or downward, to spur you on. You feel unproductive and honestly, a bit empty.

Often leaders in moments like this will say that they've never had to interview for a job in their life and that they don't even know when they wrote their last résumé. In the past they just did good work and doors continued to open for the right, next opportunity. There are so many leaders who are absorbed in their job that when they finally emerge and lift their gaze to search, they are confronted with the fact that they have a myopic network—completely internal to their last company or industry—and that they aren't as in demand as they thought. Like Eric, people outside their industry don't understand the work that they did, and recruiters and headhunters won't take the time to translate their transferable leadership skills to a different industry or sector.

Transitions are turbulent times and navigating them well is key to your success over the long haul as a leader. The life of a typical adult is full of change. Of the major decisions and transitions in life, career transitions are perhaps the most regular, life-impacting major passage. Today, people switch jobs every five years or less, making for the potential of 8–10 major role transitions over your lifetime! Long gone are the days when a leader expects to be with the same organization for the duration of their career. Even corporate leaders who stay with the same global firm for years advance by moving from one role or team to another business unit or location.

For leaders, these times of transition are also ripe for the potential of derailment. Learning effective career management skills to navigate these passages is critical to becoming a leader who lasts. It's also critical for the people you lead. Leader transitions are disruptive for the leader, but there is also a collateral impact that ripples out to the people and organizations in which you are embedded. At the heart of mastering transitions are the strategic relational investors in your trust circle who can help guide you through the steps of the process and serve as job contacts to help you bridge into your next role. Leadership transitions can feel lonely, but they don't have to be.

A Personal Board of Readiness

You don't have to navigate leadership transitions on your own. When it comes to leadership transitions, the relational investors on your personal board—your trust circle—are the key to being poised and ready for anything. The people who fill these roles for you might also occupy space in the rest of your circle. You might have a mentor or advocate who steps up in a strategic way or a family member who moves from emotional support to brokering a key introduction. This network is also made up of loose connections, people you've worked with in the past, met through conferences, or friends of friends who you get introduced to along the way.

Your career connections are critical, not just when you are looking for a job or testing the market. Many leaders have told me that they don't have time to build their career connections or that they love their role so much they don't see the value since they aren't planning to leave. These same leaders will often confess later that they didn't expect their role to change into something they never wanted. They couldn't have predicted that the organizational context would shift or that the ground underneath them in the market would be different, causing them to look for a new opportunity.

Taking a Calculated Risk

Your career connections are about the people you would call tomorrow if you were looking for a job. It's about aligning with individuals in the organizations where you would consider working who you might be willing to help you get your foot in the door. Your career connections are instrumental to landing a new job, making a successful career change, or keeping a pulse on the competitive labor market, positioning yourself for the right moment to take a leap. Don't wait to identify the relational investors who can help you navigate the ambiguity of a leadership transition.

Several years ago, I was considering leaving a steady and stable job in leadership development at a global consulting firm for an entrepreneurial adventure as the Chief Commercial Officer at WiLD Leaders, Inc. The work promised to be meaningful. The team was aligned to my values, and the methodology was cutting edge. Still, the idea of trading stability was daunting.

One reflective question from the Strategic Support Audit, an assessment in the WiLD Leaders system, posed to me in the middle of my decision provided me with a great deal of insight: "To what extent do you have the necessary strategic network in place to take a calculated risk?"[1] When I read this question, I realized that I could, in fact, take a calculated risk because I did have a strong strategic career network who'd help me develop new business for the venture. I had people who'd pick me up if I failed and needed to connect to new opportunities. Your career connections matter if you are an entrepreneur or an employee. The winds of change can carry us all.

Bad News, Good News

The bad news is that transitions are challenging. Most of us aren't quite prepared to take them on and we find ourselves getting ready in real time. The job market can be harsh, unpredictable, and confusing to navigate. Rejection is part of the game. You hear "no" more than "yes." Depending on the state of the economy, watching the news can add another layer of discouragement. A good economy makes you feel incompetent because you can't figure out why you aren't landing the right role with so much opportunity out there. A bad economy and you can get discouraged by the lack of options.

That sums up the bad news. On the other hand, there is markedly good news. Regardless of external conditions, there is nearly always someone who is looking for a leader with your skills. Even in tough markets there is always some organization that is growing, a startup receiving major funding, a not-for-profit taking in a big donation or establishing an endowment, a firm that is getting purchased, a product or service that breaks out. There is always someone looking for what you do.

If you hang around leaders in transition for a while, you'll hear about how difficult the job search process is. Ironically, if you spend time with people on the other side of the table you'll hear employers complaining about how difficult it is to find the "right" candidate for a key role. They might have a larger applicant pool but any savvy recruiter or hiring manager knows that greater quantity of candidates doesn't necessarily mean greater quality candidates. Matching employment needs to opportunities is the holy grail for hiring. It's the reason that internal recruiters and external headhunters have jobs. It's the same reason that job matching services and recruitment technology proliferate. Even in a tough job market, there is always employment churn that opens opportunities.

This means that somewhere, there is a hiring manager or board member who is feeling the pain of having a critical opening on the team. Right now, as you read this, there is a job opening that is about to be created. Someone is going to get recruited away to a competitor. Someone is going to go on parental leave and choose not to come back. Someone is going to leave and start a business. Someone is going to relocate to be closer to family. Someone is going to retire—maybe earlier than expected. Someone will get promoted or transfer to a new region. Someone is about to announce that they are following their dream to go back to school. Someone will unfortunately leave the workplace due to illness or death. Someone will step aside to take care of an aging family member. The list goes on.

Looking for the right job is hard work but it's just as difficult for organizations to find the right employees or leaders with the right skills who also align with their culture and strategic needs. Markets fluctuate but there are always opportunities being created. The overwhelmingly good news is that if you are in transition then there is someone looking for you right now. They just don't know where to find you. This means your job is to figure out how to meet them and get on the inside track—maybe even before those opportunities are formally posted on the job boards. This is what career coaches and recruiters call the "hidden" job market. It's the moment where the news about an upcoming opening is leaked and the people with a connection learn about it before it's posted on a job board for the rest of the world. This is the inside track.

The Inside Track

So how do you position yourself to get on the inside track? Every career expert will tell you to build your network. The problem is that while everybody tells you to network, no one takes the time to show you how. This whole book is about building different types of networks, diverse types of relationships for diverse challenges that we face as leaders. Hopefully you are seeing that strategic networking is so much more than merely positioning yourself to find a job.

As author Keith Ferrazzi highlights in his book, *Never Eat Alone*, networking doesn't equal job searching and job searching is about a lot more than just networking. Networking is about building relationships. It just so happens that one of the best ways to find a job—or to find a great place to eat, or even to meet that special someone—is through a circle of relationships, also known as your network.[2]

Who are the well-connected people in your circle? Who has access to information or relationships that you don't have? Who are the three names of relational investors whom you can contact today?

Connecting You to Value

There are four ways that your circle can help you in your career search. First the people in your circle can help you discover your value by asking your career connections to help you understand your differentiation—what makes you stand out—from other leaders. Second, your career network can help you define your value. Ask your career connections to review your personal brand and how you've packaged your skills in your résumé, social media profiles, portfolio, and talking points and success stories. What other assets do you need to create to define and communicate your value? Third, you can ask your career connections to help make introductions to executives who could be potential partners or employers. Who are the people they'd want to work for? What places do they keep on their own watch lists? Fourth and finally, your career network can help you deliver your value by coaching you on interviews and helping provide important information to negotiate your offer and start your new role set up for success. Your career network can help you land the job and launch well. Even if you never have to tap into your career connections, having them in place is like a relational insurance policy for your career and longevity, especially in turbulent inflection points in your business where your future is uncertain.

The Circle That Helps You Stay

The purpose of having strong, strategic career connections in place isn't just for you to land a job, it's to bolster your confidence in your ability to take calculated risks so that you can be fully invested where you are called to lead, knowing that when your time to leave comes, that you'll be able to cross the bridge to your next assignment.

Positioning yourself with your career connections isn't just about making a role change and leaving your team. Even if you don't plan to leave your organization, knowing that you have options to take a calculated risk gives you the opportunity to be at your best. When you know that your professional identity and your livelihood aren't wrapped up in—or fully dependent on—your position or organization, you have the freedom to lead without an artificial restriction.

Some of the most dangerous leaders are the ones who don't have, or don't perceive, any options for outside employment. These leaders are dangerous precisely because they have no options. Dr. Rob McKenna describes these leaders like the proverbial cat that is trapped in the corner with the choice to either cower in fear or lash out and fight back.

At best, leaders like this can feel stuck. This can look like holding onto a job longer than they should, keeping others from the opportunity to grow. Feeling stuck can also look like professional stagnation—holding back from the next opportunity to learn. At worst, these leaders are tempted to compromise their convictions for fear of what they will do next or how they will provide for themselves or their family. They are leading from a place of fear and scarcity versus service and abundance. The paradox of career connections is that having more doesn't mean you'll leave; it might be what gives you the courage and perspective to stay.

Building your career connections is strategic for you and for the organizations in which you serve by leading. The focus in this chapter is on relationships that are external to the place you work now. Internal relationships matter too, but I've seen leaders mistake a strong internal network for having a strong career network full of job contacts. Internal networks position you for promotion but aren't as helpful for external transitions.

Building your career connections is an important part of becoming a leader who will stand the test of time. We need different people, for different reasons, in different seasons. Relational investors who help you navigate leadership transitions can be one of the most important strategic investments in your career. Leadership continuity is created by career connections.

Who Would You Call Tomorrow?

Leadership transitions are disruptive moments that have the potential to make you drift toward derailment. The unexpected is going to happen. Are you ready? When done well, building career connections becomes a lifestyle habit of building generous and generative relationships—just like we saw in Chapter 3—not just a job searching activity for when things get tough.

Who would you call tomorrow if you were looking for a job? Your relational investors will be honored to serve you. Reach out to them and nurture the relationship you have. You might need them tomorrow and they might need something from you today.

Reflection Questions

- To what extent do you have the necessary strategic network in place to take a calculated risk?
- How much of your career network is concentrated in one organization? Do you have relationships in a wide range of organizations and industries?
- If you do have that strategic career network in place, how does that change the way you think about your work and your career?
- If you don't have a strategic career network in place, what is one thing you can do this week to start building it?
- Whom would you call tomorrow if you were looking for a job?

Take Action: Invest in Your Career Connectors

Your network is one of your most valuable assets, especially during times of transition. Identify the 10 people in your network who are the most well-connected. These are your most strategic connectors who can open doors for you, introduce you to new opportunities, and help you navigate your career journey.

Action Steps:

1. Create a list of your 10 most strategic career connectors. Include their current company and role.
2. Do some research on each person before meeting with them. Check their social media posts, read their recent articles or blog posts, and see what they are up to.
3. Practice being a relational investor to them. Use this research to identify ways to serve them. Maybe you can connect them with someone in your network, or maybe you can offer to help them with a project they are working on.

4. Prioritize staying in touch with each of them. Set a goal to connect with at least one of them every 4–6 weeks.

5. When you connect with your strategic connectors, be prepared to share updates about your career and any potential future aspirations you have. Most importantly, ask them questions and be more interested in their work than yours.

6. Be generous and helpful to your strategic connectors. Offer to help them in any way you can, even if it's just something small.

9

Advocates:
The Skeleton Key
to Unlock Any Door

Key Takeaways

- Advocates are the best kept secret for creating opportunity. Advocates provide you access to key information, resources, and experiences. Advocates transfer their credibility and influence to you.

- Advocates can open doors for you, break down doors for you, or create doors that you never knew existed.

- Keep an open mind. Advocates might lead you down an unexpected pathway to your goals.

- Be patient as you build advocates. Advocates are a high trust relational investor. You can't manufacture trust, it takes time.

- Advocates risk their reputation and resources on your behalf. Provide clarity about what you want and demonstrate that you are worth taking a risk on.

Sending a rocket into space takes a tremendous amount of intentionality, forethought, planning, and resources. Alongside a host of components that are required for flight, a spacecraft is typically equipped with multiple jets to propel it along its full trajectory. The rocket in the first phase does the initial work of thrusting the craft into space and out of Earth's atmosphere. This initial rocket is powerful but at a certain point its powerful thrust will only take the craft so far. At this point, a second set of rockets, the boosters, kick in and carry the spacecraft along the full continuum to its destination for exploration and discovery. Without boosters, spacecraft can make it out of the atmosphere, but they go no further. Without the critical role of the booster, a spacecraft would reach high only to float without intention.

Advocates and sponsors can play a similar role as relational investors on your circle of relational investors. The rate of your velocity and the extent of your trajectory—both in deepening your capacity as a leader or in taking on roles that stretch you to your next level—are throttled by the extent to which you have advocates to propel you to places that you want to go and to places that you couldn't imagine. Advocates can help boost you to the next level.

Sometimes described as "sponsors," your career advocates play a critical role in your network by opening opportunities to enable you to reach your goals, by creating strategic opportunities that you can't reach on your own, or by constructing possibilities that you'd never even considered before.

In this chapter, we'll look at the accelerating role of advocates and how they can open the door for sale, scale, or succession. We'll start by looking at the difference between internal advocates and external advocates. We'll then look at how advocates can open doors for you, break down doors for you, or create doors that you never knew existed. We'll end by looking at how to build strategic advocates by your side.

The Best Kept Secret

Advocates may be the relational investor that is the best kept secret of all. Advocates are often the most misunderstood and least utilized part of your trust circle. Your mentors might also advocate for you, serving in a dual role, but not always. Unlike mentoring alone, advocates may not offer timely wisdom or insights, but they do provide strategic positioning and the keys that open gateways for opportunities. Unlike job contacts, the opportunities that an advocate provides may be more expansive than merely an introduction to a hiring manager or a job lead that you then work diligently to carry to fruition. Advocates don't just open doors or provide insights about which door to open. In many cases they usher you through the doors as well, appeasing the guards and checking back to make sure you are set up for success.

If you ask a room of leaders about the people who have made the most significant impact in their careers, they usually point to mentors who have provided support or advice. It's less common for leaders to point to advocates who have intentionally chosen to leverage and risk their reputation, social capital, personal influence, resources, or positional power on a leader's behalf.

Advocates provide you access to key information, resources, and experiences. They can increase your influence through their own influence. Advocates advance your career by paving the way for a promotion or by propelling your business forward by establishing a pivotal opportunity for you with a key connection. In many cases, advocates also serve as references for your character and your performance, transferring credibility to you through their own credibility.

Internal Advocates Get the Job Done

Internal advocates are strategic relational investors for advancing within your organization or industry. David, a rising leader, was inspired to develop an analytics function in his organization that would be focused on drawing insights about the people in the business so that the organization could optimize hiring, increase retention, and build strong engagement in support of the corporate culture. David had a vision for the potential impact that this initiative would yield for his employer. The initiative also provided a key experience for him as he aimed to grow into a senior role in his team. Abdul, an executive in his firm, had the credibility and positional authority to make David's dream a reality.

David knew Abdul well enough to set up a lunch. David approached him to share the business need he'd observed and outlined a few potential approaches to developing a value-added solution. Abdul listened, affirmed David's observations, and offered his perspective as well. David took a risk and asked Abdul to help make this a reality. Abdul took a risk and expressed his willingness to "go to bat" for David with other executives, including key leaders more senior to David on his team to redirect resources and part of David's time toward the project. Abdul and David never formally called their arrangement a "sponsorship" or "advocacy," but Abdul paved the way for David to build the program he dreamed of and ensured that the project was visible to the right stakeholders in the business. Abdul's advocacy made David's project an organizational priority and positioned David as the person to lead the effort. This increased the executive team's awareness of David's skills and expanded his network across different functions in the business.

David and Abdul are a great example of the power and mechanics of advocacy. As an internal advocate, Abdul set David up for success and provided the direct influence to make it a reality, opening doors, removing barriers, and providing ongoing support to ensure that David and his project succeeded. Internal advocates like Abdul are powerful. While some organizations have formal "sponsorship" programs, many meaningful advocacy relationships happen organically when two people take a risk that is mutually beneficial.

External Advocates Make It Rain

Advocacy isn't just a relational investor for corporate leaders. If you run a business, then advocacy might be even more critical, especially if you are positioning the business for sale or looking to increase revenue. External advocacy looks a bit different than internal advocacy. The process still produces powerful acceleration for your mission in the market or in your community. Consider the people who have opened connections to clients for you. There is a difference between the people who have given you mere referrals to those who give you a recommendation, proactively endorsing your work and seeking out opportunities for you on your behalf—whether you asked them to or not. Advocates believe in your mission but most importantly they believe in you. They have the capital—either financial or social—to invest in your business, donate to your organization, or strongly encourage others to engage with you.

My father, Sam Hallak, ran a family business that provided cleaning services. Most of Sam's clients came by word of mouth, either by satisfied clients who mentioned Sam's work to friends or through happy customers who wrote a positive review of his work. These actions are meaningful but didn't quite reach advocacy. Many clients were willing to write reviews for him, but a select group of Sam's clients took their support for him to the level of advocacy. Lin was one of these customers. Lin had hired Sam's business on several occasions. She appreciated the quality his business delivered and the low-pressure sales approach so much that she took it upon herself to become his informal marketing department, proactively telling her friends that Sam was their go-to source for cleaning. Lin was also integrally connected into the Chinese American community in her region. After experiencing Sam's work several times, Lin introduced Sam to her community by serving as a conduit for trust, passing along the experience she had and ensuring and assuring that others knew that they could trust Sam because they trusted Lin. Lin didn't just refer Sam, she made intentional efforts to let her friends and family know about Sam's services even before they recognized that they needed him.

Because of Lin, Sam had dozens of new clients call and in a matter of weeks he had more than 20 new clients who hired him to serve their needs. Lin's evangelism of Sam's services made her a key client advocate of his who both passed his name along and acted as an accelerator of his work. She increased his business and opened a new community to serve, one he wasn't aware of and that he wouldn't have been able to access on his own. Her advocacy went beyond his bottom line. He was able to serve her friends and family, creating a win-win.

Advocates Are the Gatekeepers

Every relational role we've covered in this book plays a meaningful yet different part in your potential development as a leader. Advocates serve in a unique way because they often operate as gatekeepers to the developmental opportunities that catalyze people into leaders. In Chapter 2 we looked at the impact of challenging experiences as the leadership classroom where leaders are formed. These crucible moments are the place where leaders are given the opportunity to grow to the next level. If you are working to scale your business, sell your business, or identify the future leaders for your business, you are in a powerful moment of personal growth. Advocates are strategic because of the resources they can provide but also because of the opportunities and experiences that they can open with their influence.[1]

Michael Erisman is a human resources executive who is passionate about developing leaders and succession planning. Over his career, Michael has held executive level roles in numerous organizations. The breadth of Michael's experiences gives him a unique perspective on the developmental needs of an HR leader who aspired to become an executive. Michael's advocacy strategy focused on experiences. When Michael advocates for a leader, he creates opportunities for them to take on experiences that stretch them to their next level. He strategically adds key experiences to their résumé that will position them to take over a role like his one day.

Michael is credited with having minted several dozen top Chief Human Resources Executives. These are professionals whom he invested in by opening the right doors at the right time, for the right people. Advocates like Michael deliver more than mentoring and advice, although he provided that too. Advocates take risks to give you the keys to catalyst experiences that provide you the opportunity to prove yourself. Advocates like Michael do three things: (1) they open doors, (2) they break down doors, and (3) they create doors where none previously existed.

Opening Doors

One way that advocates provide strategic support is by opening doors. An advocate can position you for a key role or convince another leader to take a chance on working with you. These are the types of opportunities that you aren't quite able to reach on your own. Much like the booster rocket, the advocate takes you all the way to your destination, carrying you through to your new role and helping to ensure that you are successful. This looks like landing a promotion or securing an opportunity to lead a special project or task force.[2] These opportunities grow your influence and capacity by helping you place the next piece of the puzzle for your strategic growth.

Breaking Down Doors

Advocates open doors, but they also break down doors. Advocacy has risks for both parties; the advocate and the person being advocated for. If you have an advocate, they are taking a risk to put their reputation on the line for you. The rest of your circle of relational investors might not do that. You are also taking a risk through your openness to experiences that will stretch your comfort level. In some cases, an advocate can help propel you forward by breaking down doors that you'd already tried but weren't able to unlock on your own. Advocates knock down real and artificial barriers for your growth and development. This type of advocacy is valuable for every leader and especially for unlikely leaders who might not have all the resources, experience, or connections to break into the role that they want and need for their growth.

Creating New Doors

At the heart of advocacy relationships is trust. An advocate may have a unique perspective that you haven't considered. In some cases, advocates serve as booster rockets that take you to a destination you hadn't planned on, but when you arrive, you realize it was better than your original intention. Stephanie was growing as a leader in life sciences and expressed the desire to become an executive leader one day. Her advocate, recognizing the need for Stephanie to develop cross-functional capabilities, fought for her to get a spot in a leadership development program and to switch roles into an account manager role, working directly with customers instead of behind the scenes with the science of their business.

Stephanie couldn't see the full picture and didn't fully understand why an account focused role would set her up for success. Her advocate recognized the difficulty of climbing the ranks to executive through the science vertical and saw another pathway that wasn't clear to her. Stephanie asked questions and ultimately chose to trust her advocate and take the account management role. In the process, she developed a unique combination of technical acumen and product knowledge combined with customer relations and sales skills. This allowed her to serve clients more effectively than her peers and she outpaced their development and output. Today, Stephanie is a Vice President of Sales and Business Development, influencing the way that the science she loves is presented and positioned. Because of her technical knowledge and account management experiences, she has credibility across the organization, bridging the gap between science, production, and the consumer.

Stephanie's advocate had a vision for her that expanded what she could see herself. It was still in line with her goals, but it wasn't a clear and linear line of sight between the opportunities she stepped into and the outcomes. Stephanie reached her goal of becoming an executive, but the path looked different than she'd anticipated. In the process, she discovered new talents and interests, creating a unique and valuable skill set for her as a leader. Today, she is also positioned for the CEO role in the future based on the growing breadth of experiences that her advocate created for her.

Are You Ready?

Advocates can be a powerful strategic relationship. How do you know if you are ready for an advocate? If you want to identify an advocate to advance your development, honestly consider the commitment to decide if advocacy is what you need in this season of your life. What are you willing to sacrifice if an advocate asks you to take a risk? Advocates can open doors, but it only works when you are honest with yourself. Do you know who you are and where you want to go? Pursuing an advocate can backfire if you don't have purpose and intention driving your desire. Some leaders find that they want to advance for the sake of advancing, only to find that they've run down a path that they didn't want to go or climbed a ladder only to find themselves on a roof that they didn't want to arrive at. Why do you want to grow your business? Are you ready to sell? For the sake of what or whom do you want advocacy? Intentionality with specificity can provide an advocate with enough direction to create possibilities. You must help the advocate know how to help you.

In Stephanie's case she knew the direction she wanted to go but she was open to different pathways to get there than the conventional routes she was aware of. This is important because advocacy has risks for both parties. If an advocate is going to put their reputation or resources on the line for you, it's important for you and for the advocate that you have skin in the game and are ready to take the opportunities that they present to you.

Minimize the risk that an advocate will take to promote you by clearly communicating who you are, what you want, why you want it, and who you intend to serve. The clearer you are with your advocate, the more clearly your advocate can jointly discern if and how to strategically position you, both for your good and for the good of the people you'll grow in your capacity to lead.

If you've ever made a hasty and poor hiring decision based on a referral, then you've seen the wisdom in carefully discerning who to advocate for. Jessica was an emerging leader who was pegged as a high-potential leader by her mentor. Enthused by Jessica's aspirations and coachability, her mentor introduced her to a hiring manager she'd met. Based on the glowing recommendation, Jessica landed the job. Four months later Jessica was let go for performance problems and her mentor had to grapple with the reality that while she admired Jessica, she really hadn't seen any of her work products or witnessed her work ethic. She continued to mentor Jessica but became more thoughtful when advocating for others in the future.

I've also seen careful, thoughtful advocacy go very well for all parties. In my work with business owners through The Sage Group® and WiLD Leaders, one of the common areas I've often been called to serve is in preparing and developing leaders as part of a succession planning process. A common story is that a business owner or set of owners have grown a meaningful organization and are nearing the threshold for retirement. Wanting to preserve the value of the organization and generate future profitability, they pass the baton to either a family member or they invite members of their management team into a staged equity process to give them ownership in the company over time. Handing off their business well with leadership continuity has real financial implications but the whole story is never just about the financial transaction. The deeper story in these succession planning moments is about transferring a legacy and values. It's about preserving and evolving the place where their trusted employees and friends derive their livelihood and provide for their families. It's about a business that is often embedded in a community. Succession planning is a transfer of trust.

Trust Takes Time

I was invited to join a breakfast event that a friend of mine was hosting. At the event I sat next to a leader named Arnie Hendricks, an experienced consulting CFO who worked with multiple businesses on a part time basis to increase value, structure the sales of a business, and support strategic planning for business continuity. We struck up a conversation and discovered alignment on core values in life and business. Over the next year and a half, Arnie and I developed a relationship, and he took an interest in the WiLD Leaders methodology for leader development in a succession planning context. Over time Arnie was able to see my work and the work of my team and slowly got to know more about our heart for leaders and our capabilities for creating alignment and increasing value. One day Arnie let me know that he had several clients who needed my services. Together we discussed the needs of his clients that I could solve, and he advised me on what they might be looking for. I prepared a packet of content that demonstrated our work and Arnie followed up by setting up more than a dozen conversations with CEOs who needed my services right away or in a few months' time. Arnie took the resources I provided him and carefully constructed introductions that were personal and meaningful, showcasing our work and making a compelling reason for the leaders to work with me.

I was grateful, honored, and humbled at Arnie's generosity. When I asked him how I could serve him in return he replied that many of his clients had become friends. He cared about their success, and he cared about the people in their businesses. He told me that the best way I could serve him would be to take great care of his clients. Arnie's trust in me, built over time and punctuated by that conversation, inspired me to work with his clients and serve them with my best, caring for them and honoring him at the same time. Arnie took a risk, but it was a calculated risk that was minimized by trust and time. His advocacy came after he'd taken time to get to know my character and competence—going deeper than just merely a good vibe or a fleeting positive moment-in-time interaction. He invested the time to ensure that I was ready for his advocacy, and the result was a three-way win for myself, his clients, and himself. I was able to engage with ideal clients who I wouldn't have become aware of, he was able to add ongoing value to his trusted relationships, and his clients were able to have a key need in their businesses filled at just the right time. The best advocacy has mutual, reciprocal value. How is their advocacy of you of value to them?

One of the ways to test if you are ready for an advocate is consider what you are willing to sacrifice for an advocate for them to sacrifice on your behalf. If an advocate puts their reputation on the line, will you be willing to put in extra hours on a project, move to another part of the world, or challenge your assumptions about what growth and development looks like in your career? This type of sacrifice shouldn't be an ethical dilemma, but there often is a cost when considering an advocate. If you know you are ready, the next question you might be asking is, "How can I build an advocate?" When it comes to building advocates there are two important steps. The first is learning how to ask for advocacy and the second is learning how to demonstrate readiness so that an advocate will invest in you.

Ask for Advocacy

Sometimes we don't have advocates because we haven't asked anyone. Many leaders aren't aware of their need for advocacy or the differences between receiving advocacy and the mentorship that they've become accustomed to. Knowing what you want is critical. Asking for advocacy requires that you ask with clarity. What do you want from an advocate? What doors do you hope they will open for you? What is your desired destination that they can help you move toward? Why is it in the interest of the advocate to advocate for you? How does advocating for you advance their work or what they are invested in? These are a few of the questions to consider before you reach out to a potential advocate. Test your request on a friend and ask for feedback on how clear your request is. The clearer you are on what you want, the clearer your potential advocate will be to either take you on and invest in you or to redirect you to another leader.

Advocacy doesn't often happen by accident either; while happenstance is wonderful, the responsibility for securing an advocate rests on your shoulders. Most potential advocates are busy leading with high levels of responsibility. Getting the attention of an advocate can take a bit of time. You can celebrate if someone volunteers to advocate for you but don't wait around for it.

Demonstrate Readiness

Asking an advocate to promote you means that you are asking the advocate to take a risk on your behalf. Making your request might not be a single event but rather a series of conversations as you nurture your relationship. Demonstrating readiness is about building trust and reducing risk for your potential advocate, and yourself. Part of the process is helping the advocate to understand your story. Where you come from and where you want to go isn't always evident. Most people have a deeper story than the one listed on their résumé or bio. If you are an unlikely leader, it's important to help others know your story and to communicate the parts of your story that help an advocate know your strengths and limitations as well as the ways you'll need support. Sharing your story also builds trust. Hearing about the personal obstacles you've overcome or the source of passion and drive behind your work and leadership gives an advocate more confidence in your tenacity and willingness to do the hard work to grow.

This also underscores the importance of knowing yourself well. Your self-awareness generates confidence that you are a sure bet to invest in. It shows that you know what you want and provides clarity about what you need and if the advocate can help you or not.

It Comes Back to Trust

The more meaningful the advocacy, the greater the need for trust. If an advocate is going to break down a door for you or create one where none exists, then it's important to know that you are ready and willing to go with them. Sometimes it takes time for an advocate to see your work in action or hear about what it's like to work with you from others. Be patient and take your time. Trust isn't something that you manufacture. Trust takes time.[3] There is something for you to learn in moments of waiting. Your willingness to trust their timeline shows your advocate more of your character and what you are like when you are forced to wait patiently. This doesn't mean that you don't check in or continue to share your desires—you'll have to advocate for yourself for your advocate to advocate for you. It does mean that you'll let trust develop over time without pushing an advocate to decide something that you might both come to regret.

When an opportunity is presented, be ready to jump in and run with it. The way you respond to an opportunity will demonstrate what you will be like when further opportunities come. Also, remember that the doors that are opened for you might look different than you expect. But if you steward the opportunity well it will likely foster deeper trust and a stronger likelihood of future advocacy.

Advocates are a social resource that is often untapped. It takes intention and patience to develop advocates but the impact for you and for others can be worth it. Carefully consider your goals to discern if advocacy is what your next steps require. As you grow your influence and network, also consider whom you can advocate for. Who are the emerging or existing leaders in your life who might benefit from you taking a sacrificial risk on their behalf?

Reflective Questions

- When you consider the relationships in your circle of relational investors, why do you specifically believe you need an advocate? What purpose would an advocate fulfill?
- Where do you most need an advocate, (1) to open opportunities for you, (2) to remove barriers to opportunities for you, or (3) to suggest novel opportunities that you hadn't yet considered? Why?
- Why would another leader advocate for you, specifically? What is the value for them in advocating for you?
- What sacrifices are you willing to make for an advocate to risk their resources or reputation to open an opportunity on your behalf?
- Who are the leaders who could benefit from your advocacy on their behalf? What might it look like for you to serve them in this way?

Take Action

To make the most of advocacy relationships, start by identifying 2–3 people you believe could serve as advocates for you. Reflect on why you feel they could fill this role for you. What is it about your relationship that would make them willing to put their reputation on the line for you? Prepare a short (3–5 minutes) "pitch" of your goals and aspirations that you could use to remind your advocates of who you are and where you want to go. Reference the self-reflective prompts, template, and sample email below as a guide.

Self-Reflective Prompts
- Who are you as a leader?
- What are your goals and aspirations?
- Why do you want to achieve these goals?
- Whom do you intend to serve?
- What are you willing to sacrifice to achieve your goals?
- What specific support do you need from an advocate?

Template
- Who are you?
  - I am a [leader type] who is passionate about [your passion].
  - I have a proven track record of success in [your area of expertise].
  - I am committed to using my skills and experience to [whom you will serve].
- What do you want?
  - I want to [your goal].
  - I believe this is important because [your reason].
- Whom are you going to serve?
  - I am committed to serving [whom you will serve].
  - I believe that my work will make a positive impact on [whom you will serve].
- Why you need their help specifically
  - You have a unique [perspective/skill set/influence] in [area] that will help me achieve my goal to [your goal].
  - I trust your judgment and believe that your advice and connections will be invaluable to me.
  - I have seen you [specific example of advocate's positive impact] and believe that you can do the same for me.

- What's in it for them?
  - I believe this can help you achieve [the goals that you believe they have based on your study of their behavior].

Sample Email

Subject: Strategic Collaboration & Future Opportunities

Dear [Advocate's Name],

It was a pleasure connecting with you at [recent event where you saw them]. Our conversation regarding [shared interest or topic you discussed] sparked some further thoughts I wanted to share.

As you know, I'm deeply committed to [your passion], and my current focus is on [briefly describe your current role/projects with a focus on impact and outcomes]. Looking ahead, I'm eager to leverage my expertise to drive further impact in [general area of desired growth]. I've identified a compelling opportunity to [specific goal or type of project], and I believe this aligns well with your own strategic priorities in [mention their area of expertise/influence].

Given your exceptional track record in [area where they excel]—particularly your work on [mention a specific example of their work or impact]—I'm confident your insights would be invaluable as I develop this initiative.

Would you be available to connect briefly in the coming weeks to discuss this further? I'm certain a strategic collaboration could yield significant mutual benefits; specifically, I believe I could serve you by [insert the value that this will provide for them].

Sincerely,

[Your Name]

Conclusion: People Are the Purpose

This book is about you and it's also not about you. To become a leader who lasts, you need other people. Your performance and well-being depend on it. But it's also not about you. It's about the people whom you serve and the value you can unlock for them. As your leadership effectiveness grows, other people will receive the benefit of your maturity and development through your stable, sustaining leadership. That's because people are the purpose. Every product and service available on the market impacts people in some way, positively or negatively. The purpose of business is to catalyze human flourishing. That means that leadership is about relationships. You need relationships for your health and success and every one of the people you lead or serve needs them too.

Community isn't something nice to have, it's essential for healthy growth. You can't lead alone. If you take anything from this book, let it be this: surround yourself with relationships to help you lead well. Then take what you've learned and reinvest yourself into someone else to help them become a leader who lasts as well. Leadership isn't an individual sport; leadership is a team sport. Leadership that lasts requires us to let go of self-sufficiency and embrace interdependence on each other. It means we get vulnerable with the right people, and we humbly acknowledge our limitations. The leaders who finish the race with joy and fulfillment are the ones who are willing to ask for help along the way. They rely on other people, and they invest themselves in others as well.

In Chapter 1 we saw the incredible story of the Gund brothers whose relationship together catalyzed growth and the establishment of valuable business. Their relational DNA has become part of the culture, reflected in their employees defining the purpose of their business as to "Recognize and serve others so lives are transformed." Today, their focus is on helping steward the next generation of leaders in their business and helping teach them to nurture the same level of honest trusting relationships among themselves that the brothers had. They are giving from what they have gained. That's how relational investors work.

Building a Relational Leadership Ecosystem

This book is about building a leadership ecosystem of relational investors. Because life and leadership are full of twists and turns, you'll need different people to play different roles for you along the journey. You'll need people who challenge your assumptions, open your mind, provide you feedback, and push you to grow. These relationships provide you with *Stretch*. You'll also have moments when you need encouragement, someone to pick you up, a listening ear with no judgement or advice, a safe harbor. These are relationships that give *Support*. And then there are moments when the stakes are high, and you need connections to advocate for you and open doors. These relationships offer *Strategy*.

To build this type of relationship ecosystem requires intentionality and a commitment to community, starting with a recognition that you can't do this life alone. You really can't lead alone, so don't try to lead alone.

The beautiful thing that happens when you experience an ecosystem of relational investors is that you begin to want everyone else you know to have the same experience as well. That's where generosity infuses relationships, allowing you to give more than you get. You are building relationships for your sake, so that you can do that for the sake of others.

The leader who lasts doesn't just make it to the end of their career with a list of accomplishments on their resume and trophies on the wall. They get to reflect on a life of relationships unleashed to create value and flourishing. You take your relationships with you. This is what was most powerful about Aaron Christopher's story in Chapter 3. He realized two profound things; first, that "Relationships are everything. You cannot cut yourself off from your tribe and expect to flourish," and second, that "People deserve two things: to have fun and be loved." This guides his unique approach to creating a cultural architecture and paying more attention to making sure core values and commitments are lived in action than just the mechanics of his practice.

Using This Book to Become the Relational Investor

Now that you've reached the end of this book you can go back and choose your own adventure again. You might have read the book from cover to cover, or you simply picked the chapters you needed right now based on the assessment at the end of the Introduction. I wrote this book with the intention that you can pick it up just when you need it for the moment you are in. Now that you've reached the end, where are you today? I've included a copy of the assessment at the end of this Conclusion so that you can reflect on where you are and consider what's needed next.

When you are feeling stuck in your career, come back and read Chapters 4 and 5 on stretch and then go activate the people in your life who challenge you. When the storms of life and your career feel overwhelming, find Chapters 6 and 7 on support and find the people to help you make it through. When opportunity arises, revisit Chapters 8 and 9 on strategy and reach out to the people who can help you make the next move.

How do you become a leader who stands the test of time? The secret is simple, and the answer is right next to you: don't lead alone, build your trust circle. It's the relational secret to becoming a leader who lasts.

Take Action: Relational Investor Assessment

Directions: You need to be surrounded by a circle of relational investors to become a leader who lasts. As you consider this moment in your career as a leader, rate the extent to which you need each type of relational investor on a scale from 1–5. Add scores for each category as you go and enter them in the "Scoring Directions" at the end. Your scores on this assessment will show which relational investors are most important for you today and it will help you choose which chapters to prioritize reading first. Remember, while category is important, you need different kinds of relational investors, depending on the challenges you are facing in work or in the rest of your life.

Relational Investor Questions

1 = Not at All 2 = To a Small Extent 3 = To a Moderate Extent 4 = To a Great Extent
5 = To a Very Great Extent

STRETCH			
Feedback (Chapter 4)	• I need relational investors who give me honest, challenging, yet caring feedback.	1 2 3 4 5
	To be effective in my current leadership role and position myself for success, it's critical that. . .	
	• I increase my performance levels.	1 2 3 4 5
	• I prevent leadership derailment.	1 2 3 4 5
	• I discover my blind spots and areas for growth.	1 2 3 4 5
	Add the scores:_____	
Ideas (Chapter 5)	• I need relational investors who stimulate me to think in creative, innovative ways or to see things differently than before.	1 2 3 4 5
	To be effective in my current leadership role and position myself for success, it's critical that. . .	
	• I generate novel, creative ideas.	1 2 3 4 5
	• I initiate innovation and change.	1 2 3 4 5
	• I challenge my assumptions about how the world works.	1 2 3 4 5
	Add the scores:_____	

(continued)

Relational Investor Questions

1 = Not at All 2 = To a Small Extent 3 = To a Moderate Extent 4 = To a Great Extent
5 = To a Very Great Extent

SUPPORT

Emotional Support (Chapter 6)

- I need relational investors who I would call if my life or career were crumbling.   1   2   3   4   5

To be effective in my current leadership role and position myself for success, it's critical that. . .

- I have friendship and comradery.   1   2   3   4   5
- I increase my satisfaction in life and in my overall career.   1   2   3   4   5
- I have people whom I can confide in when things are difficult.   1   2   3   4   5

Add the scores:____

Mentors (Chapter 7)

- I need relational investors who provide important guidance in my life and career.   1   2   3   4   5

To be effective in my current leadership role and position myself for success, it's critical that. . .

- I accelerate my learning and knowledge base.   1   2   3   4   5
- I have an example of how to lead well.   1   2   3   4   5
- I increase my job satisfaction and engagement at work.   1   2   3   4   5

Add the scores:____

Relational Investor Questions

1 = Not at All 2 = To a Small Extent 3 = To a Moderate Extent 4 = To a Great Extent
5 = To a Very Great Extent

	• I need relational investors whom I will call tomorrow if I need to find a job.	1	2	3	4	5

Career Connections (Chapter 8)

To be effective in my current leadership role and position myself for success, it's critical that. . .

• I have connections who can help me to find a new job or make a career change.	1	2	3	4	5
• I stay aware of new opportunities that fit my skill set.	1	2	3	4	5
• I keep a pulse on the competitive labor market.	1	2	3	4	5

Add the scores:____

• I need relational investors who would risk their reputation on my behalf.	1	2	3	4	5

Advocates (Chapter 9)

To be effective in my current leadership role and position myself for success, it's critical that. . .

• I advance my career and land a promotion.	1	2	3	4	5
• I have access to key information, resources, or experiences.	1	2	3	4	5
• I grow my influence and reputation.	1	2	3	4	5

Add the scores:____

Scoring Directions: Add up the items in each section on the previous page. Enter the numbers under "Your Score" and then circle the category where your scores fall. This will indicate strengths and gaps in your circle of relational investors.

High Need scores in a category indicate a type of relational investor that is especially important to your effectiveness as a leader right now. This is an area to pay critical attention to. Prioritize reading the corresponding chapters right away.

Medium Need scores indicate a potential vulnerability or an untapped strength in your circle of relational investors. Prioritize high need relational investors first and read the corresponding medium need chapters for further development when you are ready.

Low Need scores indicate an area of potential stability in your circle of relational investors. This is a category of relationships that you already have in place. Read the corresponding chapters to learn how you can build on that relational stability and continue to become a leader who lasts.

Relational Investors	Your Score	What It Means (Circle the category where your score falls)		
		Low Need	Medium Need	High Need
Feedback (Chapter 4)		4–8	8–16	16–20
Ideas (Chapter 5)		4–8	8–16	16–20
Emotional Support (Chapter 6)		4–8	8–16	16–20
Mentors (Chapter 7)		4–8	8–16	16–20
Career Connections (Chapter 8)		4–8	8–16	16–20
Advocates (Chapter 9)		4–8	8–16	16–20

Notes

Introduction

1. Shen, Y., Cotton, R. D., & Kram, K. E. (2015). *Assembling your personal board of advisors*. MIT Sloan Management Review.

Chapter 1

1. Hogan, J., Hogan, R., & Kaiser, R. B. (2011). Management derailment. In S. Zedeck (Ed.), *APA handbook of industrial and organizational psychology, Vol. 3: Maintaining, expanding, and contracting the organization* (pp. 555–575). American Psychological Association.
2. Brass, D. J., Galaskiewicz, J., Greve, H. R., & Tsai, W. (2004). Taking stock of networks and organizations: A multilevel perspective. *Academy of Management Journal, 47*(6), 795–817.
3. Van Velsor, E., & Leslie, J. B. (1995). Why executives derail: Perspectives across time and cultures. *Academy of Management Perspectives, 9*, 62–72.
4. Stripling, J. (2017, June 20). *Behind a stagnant portrait of college leaders, an opening for change*. The Chronical for Higher Education.
5. Bradshaw, D. (2015, April 26). *Short tenure of deans signals a leadership void*. Financial Times.

6. Rokach, A. (2014). Leadership and loneliness. *International Journal of Leadership and Change, 2*, 6.

7. Parke, R. D., & Clarke-Stewart, K. A. (2013). Developmental psychology. In D. K. Freedheim & I. B. Weiner (Eds.), *Handbook of psychology: History of psychology* (pp. 224–247). John Wiley & Sons, Inc.

8. Yost, P. R., & Plunkett, M. M. (2011). *Real time leadership development*. John Wiley & Sons. [Chapter 9: When Leaders Derail]

9. Gabriel, A. S., Lanaj, K., & Jennings, R. E. (2021). Is one the loneliest number? A within-person examination of the adaptive and maladaptive consequences of leader loneliness at work. *Journal of Applied Psychology, 106*(10), 1517–1538.

10. Ibid.

Chapter 2

1. Bandura, A. (2001). Social cognitive theory: An agentic perspective. *Annual Review of Psychology, 52*, 1–26.

2. Wolff, H. G., & Moser, K. (2009). Effects of networking on career success: A longitudinal study. *Journal of Applied Psychology, 94*, 196–206. Wolff, H. G., & Moser, K. (2010). Do specific types of networking predict specific mobility outcomes? A two-year prospective study. *Journal of Vocational Behavior, 77*(2), 238–245.

3. Dobrow, S. R., Chandler, D. E., Murphy, W. M., & Kram, K. E. (2012). A review of developmental networks incorporating a mutuality perspective. *Journal of Management, 38*, 210–242. Vaillant, G. E. (2008). *Aging well: Surprising guideposts to a happier life from the landmark study of adult development*. Hachette UK.

4. Strauss, K., Griffin, M. A., & Parker, S. K. (2012). Future work selves: How salient hoped-for identities motivate proactive career behaviors. *Journal of Applied Psychology, 97*(3), 580–598.

5. Judge, T. A., Bono, J. E., Ilies, R., & Gerhardt, M. W. (2002). Personality and leadership: A qualitative and quantitative review. *Journal of Applied Psychology, 87*(4), 765–780.

6. Arvey, R. D., Rotundo, M., Johnson, W., Zhang, Z., & McGue, M. (2006). The determinants of leadership role occupancy: Genetic and personality factors. *The Leadership Quarterly, 17*(1), 1–20.

7. Arvey, R. D., Bouchard, T. J., Segal, N. L., & Abraham, L. M. (1989). Job satisfaction: Environmental and genetic components. *Journal of Applied Psychology, 74*(2), 187–192.
Arvey, R. D., McCall, B. P., Bouchard, T. J., Jr., Taubman, P., & Cavanaugh, M. A. (1994). Genetic influences on job satisfaction and work values. *Personality and Individual Differences, 17*(1), 21–33.

8. McCauley, C. D., Ruderman, M. N., Ohlott, P. J., & Morrow, J. E. (1994). Assessing the developmental components of managerial jobs. *Journal of Applied Psychology, 79*(4), 544–560.

9. Ibid.

10. McCall, M. W. (2010). Recasting leadership development. *Industrial and Organizational Psychology, 3*(1), 3–19.

11. DeRue, D. S., & Wellman, N. (2009). Developing leaders via experience: The role of developmental challenge, learning orientation, and feedback availability. *Journal of Applied Psychology, 94*(4), 859–875.

12. Yost, P., Bossen, M., Terrill, J., & Hallak, D. (2015). Career development in a protean world. *Unpublished manuscript*, School of Psychology, Family, and Community, Seattle Pacific University, Seattle, WA.

13. Higgins, M. C., & Kram, K. E. (2001). Reconceptualizing mentoring at work: A developmental network perspective. *Academy of Management Review, 26*(2), 264–288.

14. Hallak, D. (2014, October). Five networks to accelerate your career. *Talent Development Magazine, Association for Talent Development*, Alexandria, VA.

Chapter 3

1. Hallak, D. (2022, December). *Networking doesn't have to feel gross* [Video]. TED. https://go.ted.com/danielhallak

2. Casciaro, T., Gino, F., & Kouchaki, M. (2014). The contaminating effects of building instrumental ties: How networking can make us feel dirty. *Administrative Science Quarterly, 59*(4), 705–735.

3. Wolff, H. G., & Moser, K. (2009). Effects of networking on career success: A longitudinal study. *Journal of Applied Psychology, 94,* 196–206.
Dobrow, S. R., Chandler, D. E., Murphy, W. M., & Kram, K. E. (2012). A review of developmental networks incorporating a mutuality perspective. *Journal of Management, 38,* 210–242.

4. Casciaro, T., Gino, F., & Kouchaki, M. (2014). The contaminating effects of building instrumental ties: How networking can make us feel dirty. *Administrative Science Quarterly, 59*(4), 705–735.

5. Seligman, M. E., & Csikszentmihalyi, M. (2000). Positive psychology: An introduction. *American Psychologist, 55*(1), 5–14.

6. Cooperrider, D., & Srivastva, S. (1987). Appreciative inquiry in organizational life. In R. Woodman & W. Pasmore (Eds.), *Research in organizational change and development* (Vol. 1, pp. 129–169). JAI Press.

7. Bolino, M. C., & Grant, A. M. (2016). The bright side of being prosocial at work, and the dark side, too: A review and agenda for research on other-oriented motives, behavior, and impact in organizations. *Academy of Management Annals, 10*(1), 599–670.

8. Burg, B., & Mann, J. D. (2007). *The go-giver: A little story about a powerful business idea.* Penguin.

9. Ibid.

10. Casciaro, T., Gino, F., & Kouchaki, M. (2014). The contaminating effects of building instrumental ties: How networking can make us feel dirty. *Administrative Science Quarterly, 59*(4), 705–735.

11. Bolino, M. C., & Grant, A. M. (2016). The bright side of being prosocial at work, and the dark side, too: A review and agenda for research on other-oriented motives, behavior, and impact in organizations. *Academy of Management Annals, 10*(1), 599–670.
Castleberry, J. (2013). *The kingdom net: Learning to network like Jesus.* My Healthy Church.

Chapter 4

1. DeRue, D. S., & Wellman, N. (2009). Developing leaders via experience: The role of developmental challenge, learning orientation, and feedback availability. *Journal of Applied Psychology, 94*(4), 859–875.

2. Hogan, J., Hogan, R., & Kaiser, R. B. (2011). Management derailment. In S. Zedeck (Ed.), *APA handbook of industrial and organizational psychology* (Vol. 3, pp. 555–575). American Psychological Association.

3. Williams, J. R., & Levy, P. E. (1992). The effects of perceived system knowledge on the agreement between self-ratings and supervisor ratings. *Personnel Psychology, 45*, 835–847.

4. Kluger, A. N., & DeNisi, A. (1996). The effects of feedback interventions on performance: A historical review, a meta-analysis, and a preliminary feedback intervention theory. *Psychological Bulletin, 119*, 254–284.

5. Ashford, S. J., & Black, J. S. (1996). Proactivity during organizational entry: The role of desire for control. *Journal of Applied Psychology, 81*, 199–214.

6. Stone, D., & Heen, S. (2014). *Thanks for the feedback: The science and art of receiving feedback well (even when it is off base, unfair, poorly delivered, and frankly, you're not in the mood)*. Viking.

7. Ilgen, D. R., Fisher, C. D., & Taylor, M. S. (1979). Consequences of individual feedback on behavior in organizations. *Journal of Applied Psychology, 64*, 349–371.

8. Kluger, A. N., & DeNisi, A. (1996). The effects of feedback interventions on performance: A historical review, a meta-analysis, and a preliminary feedback intervention theory. *Psychological Bulletin, 119*, 254–284.

9. Dahling, J. J., & O'Malley, A. L. (2011). Supportive feedback environments can mend broken performance management systems. *Industrial and Organizational Psychology, 4*, 201–210.

10. Ilgen, D. R., Fisher, C. D., & Taylor, M. S. (1979). Consequences of individual feedback on behavior in organizations. *Journal of Applied Psychology, 64*, 349–371.

11. Stone, D., & Heen, S. (2014). *Thanks for the feedback: The science and art of receiving feedback well (even when it is off base, unfair, poorly delivered, and frankly, you're not in the mood)*. Viking.

12. Vroom, V. H. (1964). *Work and motivation*. Wiley & Sons.

13. Ilgen, D. R., Fisher, C. D., & Taylor, M. S. (1979). Consequences of individual feedback on behavior in organizations. *Journal of Applied Psychology, 64*, 349–371. Kluger, A. N., & DeNisi, A. (1996). The effects of feedback interventions on performance: A historical review, a meta-analysis, and a preliminary feedback intervention theory. *Psychological Bulletin, 119*, 254–284.

14. Ellis, S., & Davidi, I. (2005). After-event reviews: Drawing lessons from successful and failed experiences. *Journal of Applied Psychology, 90*, 857–871.

15. Gottman, J., Gottman, J. M., & Silver, N. (1995). *Why marriages succeed or fail: And how you can make yours last*. Simon & Schuster.

16. Ilgen, D. R., Fisher, C. D., & Taylor, M. S. (1979). Consequences of individual feedback on behavior in organizations. *Journal of Applied Psychology, 64*, 349–371.

17. Ilgen, D. R., Fisher, C. D., & Taylor, M. S. (1979). Consequences of individual feedback on behavior in organizations. *Journal of Applied Psychology, 64*, 349–371.

18. Baird, L., Holland, P., & Deacon, S. (1999). Learning from action: Embedding more learning into the performance fast enough to make a difference. *Organizational Dynamics, 27*, 19–32. Ellis, S., & Davidi, I. (2005). After-event reviews: Drawing lessons from successful and failed experiences. *Journal of Applied Psychology, 90*, 857–871.

19. Dahling, J. J., & O'Malley, A. L. (2011). Supportive feedback environments can mend broken performance management systems. *Industrial and Organizational Psychology, 4*, 201–210.

20. Ryan, R. M., & Deci, E. L. (2000). Self-determination theory and the facilitation of intrinsic motivation, social development, and well-being. *American Psychologist, 55*, 68–78.

21. Dahling, J. J., & O'Malley, A. L. (2011). Supportive feedback environments can mend broken performance management systems. *Industrial and Organizational Psychology, 4*, 201–210.

22. Kluger, A. N., & DeNisi, A. (1996). The effects of feedback intervention on performance: A historical review, a meta-analysis, and a preliminary feedback intervention theory. *Psychological Bulletin, 119*, 254–284.

23. Kluger, A. N., & DeNisi, A. (1996). The effects of feedback intervention on performance: A historical review, a meta-analysis, and a preliminary feedback intervention theory. *Psychological Bulletin, 119*, 254–284.

Chapter 5

1. Columbia Business School. (n.d.). *Does the rise of AI compare to the Industrial Revolution? 'Almost...'* Columbia Business School Research Brief. Retrieved January 12, 2025, from https://business.columbia.edu/research-brief/research-brief/ai-industrial-revolution.

2. McDonald, M. L., Khanna, P., & Westphal, J. D. (2008). Getting them to think outside the circle: Corporate governance, CEOs' external advice networks, and firm performance. *Academy of Management Journal, 51*(3), 453–475.

3. Agrawal, A., Goldfarb, A., & Oettl, A. (2019). Social networks and invention. *American Economic Review, 109*(4), 1480–1511. Granovetter, M. S. (1973). The strength of weak ties. *American Journal of Sociology, 78*(6), 1360–1380.

4. Burt, R. S. (2004). Structural holes and good ideas. *American Journal of Sociology, 110*(2), 349–400.

5. Amabile, T. M. (1998, September-October). How to kill creativity. *Harvard Business Review, 76*(5), 76-87. Perry-Smith, J. E., & Mannucci, P. V. (2017). From creativity to innovation: The social network drivers of the four phases of the idea journey. *Academy of Management Review, 42*(1), 53-79.

6. Baer, M. (2010). The strength-of-weak-ties perspective on creativity: A comprehensive examination and extension. *Journal of Applied Psychology, 95*(3), 592–601.

7. PATH. (n.d.). *Who we are.* Retrieved January 12, 2025, from https://www.path.org/about/who-we-are/

8. Nickerson, R. S. (1998). Confirmation bias: A ubiquitous phenomenon in many guises. *Review of General Psychology, 2*(2), 175–220.

9. Gerber, M. E. (2007, May). How to build a successful peer advisory group. *Harvard Business Review, 85*(5), 124-127.

Chapter 6

1. DeRue, D. S., & Wellman, N. (2009). Developing leaders via experience: The role of developmental challenge, learning orientation, and feedback availability. *Journal of Applied Psychology, 94*(4), 859–875.

2. Rokach, A. (2014). Leadership and loneliness. *International Journal of Leadership and Change, 2,* 6–12.

3. Deci, E. L., & Ryan, R. M. (2002). Overview of self-determination theory: An organismic dialectical perspective. In E. L. Deci & R. M. Ryan (Eds.), *Handbook of self-determination research* (pp. 3–33). University of Rochester Press.

4. Vaillant, G. E. (2008). *Aging well: Surprising guideposts to a happier life from the landmark study of adult development.* Hachette UK.

5. Parke, R. D., & Clarke-Stewart, K. A. (2013). Developmental psychology. In D. K. Freedheim & I. B. Weiner (Eds.), *Handbook of psychology: History of psychology* (pp. 224–247). John Wiley & Sons, Inc.

6. Haney, C. (2018). The psychological effects of solitary confinement: A review of the literature. *American Journal of Public Health, 108*(6), 730–740.
Shalev, S. (2009). A source of psychological trauma: Solitary confinement in the prison system. *The Lancet, 373*(9666), 1018–1021.

7. Vaillant, G. E. (2008). *Aging well: Surprising guideposts to a happier life from the landmark study of adult development.* Hachette UK.

8. Crabb, L. (1997). *Connecting: A radical new vision.* Word Publishing.

9. Van Emmerik, I. H. (2004). The more you can get the better. *Career Development International, 9*(6), 578–594.

Chapter 7

1. National Institute for Health Research. (n.d.). *Maintaining momentum in mentoring relationships.* Retrieved from https://www.nihr .ac.uk/maintaining-momentum-mentoring-relationship.

2. Ragins, B. R., & Kram, K. E. (2007). The roots and meaning of mentoring. In *Handbook of mentoring at work* (pp. 3–15). SAGE Publications.

3. Allen, T. D., Eby, L. T., Poteet, M. L., Lentz, E., & Lima, L. (2004). Career benefits associated with mentoring for protégés: A meta-analysis. *Journal of Applied Psychology, 89*(1), 127–136.
Eby, L. T., Allen, T. D., Evans, S. C., Ng, T. W., & DuBois, D. L. (2013). Does mentoring matter? A multidisciplinary meta-analysis comparing mentored and non-mentored individuals. *Journal of Vocational Behavior, 83*(1), 1–14.

4. Allen, T. D., Eby, L. T., Poteet, M. L., Lentz, E., & Lima, L. (2004). Career benefits associated with mentoring for protégés: A meta-analysis. *Journal of Applied Psychology, 89*(1), 127–136.

5. Avolio, B. J., Walumbwa, F. O., & Weber, T. J. (2009). Leadership: Current theories, research, and future directions. *Annual Review of Psychology, 60*, 421–449.

6. Holt-Lunstad, J., Smith, T. B., Baker, M., Harris, T., & Stephenson, D. (2015). Loneliness and social isolation as risk factors for mortality: A meta-analytic review. *Perspectives on Psychological Science, 10*(2), 227–237.

7. Murphy, A. L. (2012). Reverse mentoring at work: Fostering cross-generational learning and developing millennial leaders. *Academy of Management Perspectives, 26*(4), 16–29.

8. Eby, L. T., Allen, T. D., Evans, S. C., Ng, T., & DuBois, D. L. (2008). Does mentoring matter? A multidisciplinary meta-analysis comparing mentored and non-mentored individuals. *Journal of Vocational Behavior, 72*(2), 254–267.

9. Kram, K. E. (1985). *Mentoring at work: Developmental relationships in organizational life.* Glenview, IL: Scott, Foresman.

10. Ensher, E. A., & Murphy, S. E. (2011). The mentoring relationship challenges scale: The impact of mentoring stage, type, and gender. *Journal of Vocational Behavior, 79*(1), 253–266.

11. Quinn, J. (2012). *Mentoring: Progressing women's careers in higher education*. Equality Challenge Unit.

Chapter 8

1. McKenna, R. (n.d.). *Strategic support assessment [Assessment]*. WiLD Leaders Inc.

   McKenna, R. (n.d.). *WiLD profile [Assessment]*. WiLD Leaders Inc.

2. Ferrazzi, K. (2005). *Never eat alone: And other secrets to success, one relationship at a time*. Doubleday.

Chapter 9

1. King, Z. (2017). The role of sponsorship in leadership development. *Industrial and Organizational Psychology, 10*(1), 102–105.

2. Ibarra, H., Carter, N. M., & Silva, C. (2010). Why men still get more promotions than women. *Harvard Business Review, 88*(9), 80–85.

3. Lewicki, R. J., & Bunker, B. B. (1996). Developing and maintaining trust in work relationships. In R. M. Kramer & T. R. Tyler (Eds.), *Trust in organizations: Frontiers of theory and research* (pp. 114–139). Sage Publications.

Build Your Trust Circle, Your Business, and Your Future

A strong Trust Circle is the foundation of a successful career, a valuable business, and a high-trust, high-performance culture. Now it's time to turn insight into action.

Email Info@The-Sage-Group.com to work with Daniel and his team at The Sage Group® to:

Grow the Value of Your Business

Are you ready to grow the value of your business and prepare for a successful, strategic exit? Let's build your personalized Path to Value™ for you, your leadership team, and your business.

Measure Trust and Lead Through Change

Trust is the currency of change. Use the WiLD Trust Index and build a high-trust, high-performance culture inside your team or organization.

Book Daniel Hallak for Your Next Event

If you want a keynote or workshop that's dynamic, memorable, and packed with practical takeaways, visit www.DanielHallak.com to invite Dr. Daniel Hallak to speak at your next event. Explore his signature talks and unlock additional tools and resources that will take your experience with this book even further.

Acknowledgments

Writing acknowledgments for a book about relational investors in your life is no small feat! I've been honored to have dozens of people invest in me over the years. A co-worker once told me that I collected mentors like baseball cards. Relationships are the reason I've been able to do anything of meaning and value. Below is only a sample of the people who have made a meaningful impact in my life as part of my own trust circle. You have made a mark in my life. Thank you.

- My late father, Sam Hallak. For believing in me and always reminding me that, "These are the best days of your life" and that, "You got this, dads!" I wish I could share this book with you in its finished form.
- To my mom, Susan Hallak, for being such a great role model and being the first person to be there for me. For my brothers, Alex and Michael, for taking interest in this project and ideating with me and for being "the original" trust circle.
- My in-laws, Eric and Dana Critchlow, for all their support over the years and to Eric for being a second father to me.
- My kids for giving me the motivation to do work that matters. For letting me write at night and on the weekends and for asking about my book and telling your friends. I want you to grow up with the right people around you to unleash your potential and teach you how to love others well. I'm always in your corner.

- To my team at The Sage Group®, Ron Worman, Alan Andersen, and Matt Skarin and our network partners. You all live this book with me daily with your relational investment in me and in the way that you invest in our clients so deeply through our Path to Value™ Methodology as advisors, leaders, mentors, cheerleaders, coaches, and true partners. Your covenantal brotherhood goes beyond business. Ron, thank you for inviting us into this adventure and for helping turn your wisdom, experience, and the scars on your back into a valuable business for us as we take the next generation of The Sage Group® forward. I promise to pass on the lessons you've passed on to us.

- To Alan and Sarah Andersen, Jairis and Stephanie Laurie, and Brian and Elisa Hope for being the type of friends that can show up in a crisis or relax on the patio with you. Our entire family is blessed by your family. You are the manifestation of the heart of this book.

- Rob McKenna and Paul Yost for first introducing me to the concept of a developmental network and a strategic board of advisors. For inviting me to earn a PhD and changing my name in the process. To Rob for being able to live this out as a member of the WiLD Leaders executive team as we supported each other and "went to battle together" and impacted thousands of people in the process. I stand on the shoulders of giants.

- Brian Hope for the weekly reminders of the good news and for the many "walk and talks" with perspective, wise counsel, and practical tools and reminders of what's mine to hold and what's not. I'm grateful for you.

- Matt Youngquist for his in-depth mentoring in the career development field in my early career. Matt opened his entire business and frameworks to me and guided me on issues from pricing to helping clients change. He was one of the first people to reframe networking for me as a lifestyle, not an action.

- To my friends who read the early drafts of this book and gave me transformational feedback: Ben Brock, Claire Jenkins, Megan Lawrence, John Rogers, Cory Hartman, Chris Kelnhofer, Paul Jessup, and Chip MacGregor. You will see your input throughout this book!

- To all my students from Seattle Pacific University, Bellevue College, and California Baptist University. This book is a collection of the messages I've given you over the years so that you can become a leader who lasts. Many of these themes were tested and proved with you in your careers. I'm honored that many of you still call me to check in and get advice.

- The mentors who have spoken into my life in different seasons for different reasons: Jeff Rogers, Denise Daniels, Al Erisman, Gary Karns, Adam Sinnett, David Parker, Steve and Julie Poole, Massimo Backus, Cheryl Vermilyea, Joey Collins, Dana Kendall, Matt Nelson, Jonathan Alexander, Jonathan Catherman, Mark Vincent, and Hank Floyd. And the countless mentors whom I've missed.

- The leaders whose stories have inspired me into the pages of this book. Thank you for sharing your stories: Graeme Weston, Kathy Thaut, Rich and Steve Gund, Lauren Rogers, Alex Boyd, Aaron Christopher, Chris Nicholas, Brad Jackson, Greg Leith, Dave Gartenberg, Matt Groshong, Al Erisman, Michael Erisman, Arnie Hendricks, and many others whose names have been altered for confidentiality.

- Finally, the leaders and owners who have trusted me with their businesses as my clients. I am called to serve leaders who believe that people are the purpose and you live it out and teach me through your convictions and servant leadership. I am honored to play many of the roles in this book in your lives and businesses and to help you to do that for the people you are called to care for. Relationships are the heart of this book and that is my deepest desire for you and the most enduring wealth I can help you create. Thank you for inviting me into your circle.

About the Author

Daniel Hallak is a partner and strategic advisor at The Sage Group® where he leads the human capital efforts in The Path to Value™ Methodology. Daniel has also served as the Chief Commercial Officer at WiLD Leaders, a company that pioneered the ability to measure and build trust, tying people and performance together. He continues to serve WiLD as a strategic integrator. Daniel is also a Founding Member and facilitator of the SageGroup Collective, a just-in-time advisory board of storied executives and advisors that assembles to help leaders solve their most complex challenges. Daniel specializes in connecting strategy, execution, and leadership development to create high-performance cultures of trust and highly differentiated market value. His experience working with CEOs and business owners during critical inflection points, such as scaling, selling, or planning for succession, has given him unique insight into the triumphs and trials of leadership transitions. Daniel is known for his relationship-centered approach that is captured in his popular TEDx, *Networking Doesn't Have to Feel Gross* (go.ted.com/danielhallak). He believes that people are the purpose of business, and that genuine, generous relationships are the key to unlocking lasting value. With a PhD in Industrial-Organizational Psychology, Daniel brings a research-based discipline to his work.

Index